LILIES

LILIES

beautiful varieties for home and garden

NAOMI SLADE

photography by

GEORGIANNA LANE

GIBBS SMITH
TO ENRICH AND INSPIRE HUMANKIND

Contents

INTRODUCTION

ALMOST IMPOSSIBLY EVOCATIVE, THE LILY IS A FLOWER WITH A THOUSAND
TALES TO TELL. IT IS A SYMBOL OF SEX AND PASSION, OF GODDESSES
AND VIRGINS. A SIGN OF ABUNDANCE AND PURITY IN THE HANDS OF A
BRIDE, IT CAN ALSO BE TORRID, DIVISIVE AND CAPRICIOUS. IT DELIGHTS
IN COMPLEXITY AND FREQUENTLY MANAGES TO BE SEVERAL THINGS AT
ONCE, YET ITS FABULOUS FRAGRANCE AND SYBARITIC GOOD LOOKS HAVE
RENDERED IT ICONIC ACROSS THE GLOBE.

Lilies are familiar because they are ancient. Evolving before the very dawn of mankind, they were poised at our own birth to catch, embrace and captivate us. Despite the innocent blooms that dance in the wilderness, they tend to be portentous rather than frivolous, and they are never cozy. Adopted by religion, death and politics, the lily is a plant of ritual significance and multifaceted symbolism.

Yet they are undeniably beautiful and, more than that, they are useful in myriad ways. As the prairie harvest of the Native Americans and a dinner-table staple in China; employed in an ointment for footsore Roman soldiers and medieval cures for baldness; included in bouquets and in funeral wreaths for that perfume, so coquettish and seductive, that also masks so well the stench of death.

The early history of mankind is inscribed in pictures. Art, sculpture and other forms of graphic representation frequently outlast fragile texts, and the earliest images of lilies are Minoan, relics of a civilization that flourished between 3000 and 1100 BCE. We know they are lilies; we can see them. But when it comes to the written word, the story starts to come unstuck.

In his Sermon on the Mount, Jesus says: "Consider the lilies of the field, how they grow; they toil not, neither do they spin" (Matthew 6:28). Here, Jesus encapsulates the flower as a beautiful, relatable symbol of faith – why, after all, should we concern ourselves with raiment and sustenance when all of nature is in the hands of a merciful God?

Although delivered by God's own public speaker, this is an evocative metaphor by any measure; after all, we know lilies, do we not? Their beauty, their elegance, their simplicity and their perfume?

But presume to consider them properly, interrogate them, even, and it soon becomes evident that lilies represent something very complex indeed. The plant itself, its relationship with mankind throughout history, its social and religious significance, and even its horticulture are not quite the image of simplicity that is implied in this biblical quote.

Even if taken literally, the passage could refer to almost any flower endemic to that region. The lily as an all-encompassing shorthand for the flowers, or even the beasts, of the field. A charming allegory in a sermon without footnotes.

As gardeners we also do our best to confuse ourselves, and a number of plants are recognized as lilies – water lilies, Guernsey lilies, trout lilies, calla lilies, plantain lilies, lilies of the valley. Meanwhile, within the Family *Liliaceae*, are foxtail lilies (*Eremurus*) and pagoda lilies (*Erythronium*), as well as fritillaries and tulips. Yet, here too, we must cast these false lilies aside: this book concerns true lilies, the genus *Lilium*.

The very first lilies arose in a place in East Asia, around 19.5 million years ago; a point when primitive African primates were not yet apes and early hominids were just a faint twinkle in the eye of evolution.

Aeons passed and mountains rose; continents were torn apart and new ones created. In geological time the world is far from static, and as tectonic collisions built the Himalayas, the mountains profoundly impacted global weather systems, particularly monsoon patterns and periods of glaciation.

The proto-lily, minding its own business in a quiet corner of Asia, found its whole landscape rippling imperceptibly upwards. Plants that had evolved relatively close to sea level were suddenly thrust into the sky. Divided from their fellows by new mountains, glaciers and oceans, populations split into different lineages and diverged into various species in response to the changing landscape and climate.

With the Anthropocene, the ascent of lilies could be charted via art and cultural tradition. The Cretan walls entombed in volcanic ash, the petrified Ancient Egyptian perfumiers, the Assyrian bas-reliefs and the Roman funerary engravings appearing, over millennia, from Persia to the Far East. In the West, meanwhile, the hagiographic iteration and reiteration of the symbolic lily would verge on the tedious – if the art in question was not all so very beautiful.

White lilies shook off the taint of Roman and pagan associations to become the icons of Easter and representations of the Madonna, springing miraculously from the tears of Eve or Christ. The Annunciation was a rich source of inspiration during the Renaissance, with occasional, spine-chilling asides where Christ is seen nailed to a cross made of lilies, and the Pre-Raphaelite artists continued the theme. Rossetti's depiction of Mary as a cowering teenager receiving lilies from the Archangel Gabriel in *Ecce Ancilla Domini!*, and John Singer Sargent's famous *Carnation, Lily, Lily, Rose*, are delivered with the customary vivid sensuality of the age.

Notwithstanding the many woodcuts and illustrations in florilegia, herbals and botanical texts through the ages, the Dutch Masters painted their lilies in absorbing detail and the flower was a popular motif in Victorian and Arts and Crafts wallpaper.

The poetry of lilies is usually sensuous or mournful – when it is not self-indulgent or excessive. Regrettably frequently, the quality of the tribute does not match its peerless subject. But exceptions include the work of Tennyson, Marvell and Keats, and the lily, almost inevitably, became the signature flower of that notoriously flamboyant rhymer and rake, Oscar Wilde.

What is intriguing, though, is the degree to which people see what they want to see – embracing purity and ignoring perversion; acknowledging the light without the dark. Those who cheerfully quote the Song of Solomon (2:1): "I am the rose of Sharon, and the lily of the valleys," unaccountably overlook the frankly erotic phrases that appear later in the text, concerning "lips like lilies, dropping sweet-smelling myrrh" (5:13) and references to breasts like young deer feeding among the lilies.

Although Christianity sought to make the flower its own, earlier gods used and abused lilies to their own ends, and mythological references are legion. According to Greek legend, the first lilies sprang from the breast of Hera. Homer wrote that Persephone was gathering irises, violets and lilies when she was abducted by Hades.

Meanwhile, in the hands of Aphrodite and her darker Roman counterpart, Venus, lilies were the target of jealousy and spite. According to Roman mythology, as Venus rose from the sea, she saw a flower so fair and delectable as to rival her own charms. Consumed with envy, she caused a large, phallic pistil to spring from its center, ruining its looks and linking both flower and deity with satyrs, the personification of lust.

Yet this is refreshing. Lily lore is littered with references to the worship of women, their purity and virginity, their symbolic bridal deflowering and their fertility or abundance. One starts to wonder if the lily has been hijacked by the cloying forces of social puritanism. A flower of symbolic, unattainable perfection that links a woman's worth to both her chastity and her ability to breed.

Feisty, jealous goddesses, with their petty and vengeful ways, are more relatable. While they did concern themselves with fertility, they largely ignored purity. They bore children and behaved badly. They fraternized and fornicated with gods and mortals alike in an anarchic ownership of their sexuality, while reserving the right to anger and to take unsentimental, decisive action – against even flowers, if necessary – to protect their interests. The ultimately powerful female role models of their age.

For me, lilies are much more than just a flower. Tracing their passage through layered time is fascinating; trying to make sense of their multiple personalities leaves me with the sense that, in the mirror ball of the human psyche, they have transcended their own symbolism, become anything we want them to be: pure and luminous or dark and dirty, as required. The embodiment both of hope and salvation and of something else, far more terrifying. A beautiful, monstrous and divisive flower – an idol that is as anthropomorphically complex as any of the deities that claim it.

In the world of horticulture, though, the lily represents a different sort of religion. One is transported by the wave of joy and esteem; one can enjoy, vicariously, the enthusiasm of even the most experienced growers. It is a world where the collection and hybridization of lilies has yielded its own gods, people with as much personality and *joie de vivre* as the plants they grew.

This is a book for pleasure, and although I favor quiet, dainty, wild-type plants, all lilies have their fans – no matter how brash, bold or overwhelmingly fragrant they may be. And should the appetite for *Lilium* be whetted, there are many other books to inspire and guide the novice through this bewildering and arcane floral landscape. The legions of tigers and leopards, Trumpets and Aurelians, the Stargazers, the doubles and singles, Asiatics, Orienpets, orchids and everything in between.

When scientist J.B.S. Haldane was asked what his studies had taught him about the nature of the Creator, he responded: "That God has an inordinate fondness for stars and beetles." Given their myriad nature, it seems highly likely that He has a fondness for lilies, too.

THE HISTORY AND BOTANY OF LILIES

From the rocky coast of Japan to the moist meadows of North America, the summer air is fragrant with lily flowers. It is a plant of profound familiarity, chiming deep within our souls, delighting endlessly in its elegance and beauty and fundamentally embedding itself into human consciousness. With a history extending back to the dawn of mankind, the lily has walked every step of our evolution with us, yet continues to morph and surprise.

Lilies need no introduction. They grace our bouquets and churches; they are a cottage-garden staple, an artistic metaphor and the stuff of legend. They are flowers imbued with joy and significance, yet have hidden depths and carry with them a sense of revelations still to come.

True lilies are herbaceous flowering plants belonging to the genus *Lilium*. Of approximately 115 lily species and 80–100 sub-species known today, more than half are native to China and East Asia, while others are found in the Caucasus, southern Europe and North America, although wild populations are often threatened by human expansion and indiscriminate collecting.

Having diverged significantly over time and distance, individual species often occupy quite limited ranges. Yet evolution has rendered them versatile; lilies can be found on rocky mountain crags and alpine meadows, in wetlands, prairies, forests and coasts. The flowers may be bold trumpets or dainty bells, attracting bees, butterflies, moths and even hummingbirds to their liberal pollen and irresistibly juicy nectaries.

Lilies in antiquity

Fragrant, spectacular and, above all, edible, lilies would have appealed immediately to early humans, and because of this they have been foraged or farmed as a food crop by the indigenous populations of North America and East Asia. But as societies evolved and developed complex traditions of art, ritual and ornamental horticulture, the showy flowers attained yet further significance and worth.

When archaeologists explored the Minoan Palace of Knossos, in Crete, in the early twentieth century, they uncovered a throne room adorned with lilies and gryphons. Nearby, "the Lily Prince" strode across a wall in glorious array, wearing a crown of lilies and peacock feathers and with a wreath of lilies around his neck. Another frieze, showing lilies growing in a rocky landscape, was also exposed on the Minoan island of Thera – now Santorini.

In 1932, a high-class villa in Amnisos, Crete, was excavated, which became known as The

House of the Lilies for its fresco featuring mint, irises and papyrus, together with white *Lilium candidum* and red *L. chalcedonicum*. The earliest archaeological example yet found, it dates to between 1600 and 1500 BCE. In all cases, the locations of these images suggest a link with power, or aspirations thereof, and there may also have been a ritual significance. So, for at least 3,500 years, lilies have been cherished and cultivated around the Mediterranean and along the lines of the ancient Empires. Making their way gradually into gardens, they were doubtless joined on occasion by other European natives, such as *L. martagon* and perhaps the widespread *L. pyrenaicum*, under the radar of the botanical establishment. And, through rituals of our own, a handful of lily varieties have leapt to modern prominence.

A FLOWER OF MOURNING

In many cultures, flowers are part of the rituals of death. The brief moment of brilliance before they fade and decay is a compelling metaphor for our own existence. And although garlands have been discovered in Ancient Egyptian pyramids, the earliest, most atavistic floral tribute was discovered in Israel, where the excavation of an ancient grave revealed that the occupants had been laid to rest on a bed of wild flowers, more than ten thousand years ago.

If lilies were included then, it was surely incidental, yet it is a flower that has since become irrevocably associated with funerals in a history that can be traced from images of lilies on Minoan funerary caskets, and the massed blooms that accompanied Roman ceremonies, to the flowers that honor the dead today. And it may not be irrelevant in relation to the tradition of associating white flowers with death. Snowdrops, for example, have been described as looking "like a corpse in its shroud" and the hawthorn tree, *Crataegus monogyna*, has flowers that are traditionally associated with misfortune and carry a faint scent of putrescence.

But lilies, with their complex backstory of abundance and purity, sex and death – and being already symbolic – are obvious candidates for the task. Deeply appropriate for the graves of innocents and also to indicate a soul washed clean of sin is ascending to a higher place. Meanwhile, here on Earth, the strong, sweet scent would have been effective in masking the odor of decay.

Today, funeral flowers are big business, and while these are associated with white lilies, grieving relatives often choose anything but. Fashion, too, dictates new traditions: in the floristry lexicon, Stargazer lilies are said to represent sympathy and Oriental lilies eternal life. But the classic white bloom remains modest, mournful and, in most places in the world, unquestionably suitable for the occasion.

The rise of the Madonna lily

Prominent since antiquity, as we have seen, beautiful *Lilium candidum* stands out as the symbolic lily of choice. The blooms are large and fragrant; they are clear white and carried proudly erect on stately stems. They radiate untouchable purity and innate holiness, and they are the obvious choice of flower for virgins and goddesses.

As an ancient symbol of the passage from innocence to adulthood, lilies were often included in a bridal bouquet, and in Minoan Thera, the characteristics of *L. candidum* and *L. chalcedonicum* are seen stylistically combined in paintings that were found in a room for ceremonies. It is thought that these could have included wedding rituals, linked with the worship of the local vegetation goddess. The theology of the Mediterranean and the Near East is complex and layered, but this deity of creation, fertility, virginity, sex – and even war – may be a precursor of similar goddesses of the wider region, including Ishtar, Astarte or Inanna; suggesting that, even from an early point, the deity might evolve but the lily remains symbolically significant.

Several thousand years later, the lily appears in Ancient Greek and Roman mythology, linked variously to Persephone and Aphrodite or Venus. But, above all, it was the flower of the Queen of the Gods – Hera in Greece and Juno in Rome. In Greek legend, Zeus brought the son he had fathered with a mortal woman to sup at the divine breast of Hera, whom he had drugged. On awakening, the appalled goddess threw the baby from her; causing milk to spray across the sky and the Earth, where it formed the Milky Way and sprang into bloom as lilies.

The mirror of history is clouded and when it comes to ancient lilies people speak as they find. It has been suggested that the "lilies" of Thera and Crete might actually be *Pancratium maritimum*, the beautiful and fragrant sea daffodil. Similarly, there are theories that the bloom that was so furiously defaced by Venus (see page 11), was not *L. candidum* but the infinitely more phallically endowed calla lily, *Zantedeschia aethiopica*. But whatever the truth, large, white lily flowers evidently capture human imagination.

The advent of Christianity brought its own image of feminine heavenly purity, and the Virgin Mary was represented from an early point by roses and lilies – at first red, but later white. And, as the Madonna lily, *L. candidum* has now overwhelmingly been adopted as the symbol of the Mother of Christ.

So, *L. candidum*, well established as an icon of purity and fertility, takes on a new kind of ecclesiastical heft. Lilies are referred to in both Christian Testaments; the Venerable Bede (c.673–735 CE) described ardently its chaste petals and the divine light emanating from the anthers at its core. As Christianity dominated its pagan predecessors, the new religion adopted a range of conventions, such as feast days, from the old religions, and it is interesting to consider lilies in the context of such a conflation.

There is the dual symbolism: the flower that simultaneously represents purity and fecundity. There is the repeated theme of a virgin birth or, rather, a miraculous, immaculate conception. Hera, frustrated by the philandering of Zeus, also conceived a son, Hephaestus, alone. Unmarried Mary, meanwhile, is surprised by the Archangel Gabriel, who tells her she will bear the son of God.

By the Renaissance, the lily was secure in Christian symbolism. In Leonardo da Vinci's *Annunciation* (c.1472), the angel appears holding a miraculously out-of-season Madonna lily, but about thirty years earlier, Giovanni di Paolo painted the Archangel Michael expelling Adam and Eve from an Eden filled with fruit, roses and lilies. Thus both artists assured the position of *L. candidum* as not just the Madonna lily, borne by angels, but a true flower of paradise.

EASTER LILIES

When Swedish naturalist Carl Peter Thunberg discovered *Lilium longiflorum* in 1777 in southern Japan, he could never have known that it was destined for glory. Biding its time, the flower headed west to Europe before hitching a ride to Bermuda, where it changed its name, winning hearts and minds and being grown in huge numbers as the Bermuda Lily, until the crop was struck with a virus and production reverted to Japan.

But by then Easter lilies had already broken America: in Christian tradition, when Christ was crucified, lilies grew where His blood and tears fell. So, churches and altars are adorned with white lilies to celebrate the resurrection; glorious trumpets to herald new life and hope, and spring itself.

In the 1880s, a Mrs Thomas Sargent was visiting Bermuda when she spied a display of wonderful flowers. Captivated, she carried some home to Philadelphia and gave a few to a local nurseryman, William Harris, who saw their potential. Superficially similar to Madonna lilies, these flowers could be forced to bloom in March or April and they became increasingly popular, eventually becoming synonymous with Easter – in the USA, at least.

The bombing of Pearl Harbor in 1941 put an abrupt end to trade between Japan and America, and the price of Easter lilies rocketed. But, serendipitously, a new supply of the nation's favorite flower presented itself.

When soldier Louis Houghton returned from the First World War he had brought with him a suitcase of *L. longiflorum* bulbs for his gardening friends in Oregon. These amateur lily growers suddenly found themselves with a profitable enterprise: lilies were dubbed "White Gold," and business boomed. By 1945 there were an estimated 1,200 lily growers in the region and it remains a center of large-scale production.

But before *L. longiflorum*, there was a pretender to the throne, in the form of *Zantedeschia aethiopica*, the calla lily or arum lily, which was grown in great quantity in Victorian times. In the 1920s, this earlier Easter lily also became the symbol of remembrance of the Republican combatants that died in the Easter Rising of 1916 in Dublin, and the motif has remained significant in the Irish community ever since.

ORANGE LILY OF POLITICS

Native to Europe and a garden staple for hundreds of years, *Lilium bulbiferum* has generously contributed its genes to the palimpsest of Asiatic lilies that we enjoy today. Naturalized in the Netherlands, it is known locally as the herring lily, or *roggelelie* – the rye lily. Yet, through no fault of its own, it has become politically notorious.

Due to its color it was adopted as a symbol of William III, Prince of Oranje-Nassau, or William of Orange, as he is also known, and it is featured in a portrait of the young prince that dates from the 1660s. With his wife Mary he became joint ruler of England, Ireland and Scotland and lived ostentatiously at Hampton Court Palace, in Surrey.

In the Battle of the Boyne, in July 1690, between the forces of Protestant William III and Catholic former king, James II, the Protestants were victorious and the July-flowering lily took on a new significance. When the Orange Order was formed at the end of the eighteenth century, they embraced this symbol, along with the flowers of sweet William, and instigated an annual parade on 12 July to celebrate the victory. The Catholic and Protestant conflict simmered on in "The Troubles," which were eventually resolved in the Good Friday Agreement in 1998.

Into the garden

By and large, cultivated plants move naturally by a process of diffusion, slowly, passed from individual to individual: but when politics gets involved, this can change dramatically. When great nations form alliances or expedience sees colonists, explorers, missionaries or collectors punch their way into new territories, almost anything that returns down the line is liable to be valued as a treasure or, at least, a fashionable novelty worth acquiring.

In the sixteenth century, diplomatic amity broke out between the Holy Roman Empire of Western Europe, based in Vienna, and the Ottoman Empire centered in Constantinople, where Ogier Ghiselin de Busbecq was ambassador between 1554 and 1562. Astonished by the gardens he found, he brought back many unusual bulbs, including Turkish native *Lilium chalcedonicum*. The petals of this variety curl backwards to create a rounded shape, a little like a turban, and it may be the flower that inspired the common name of "Turk's cap lily."

With the colonization of the Americas, more new lilies began to emerge. In the early 1600s, French settlers in Canada sent elegant, willowy *L. canadense* to Europe and this was followed by other American species; towering swamp lily, *L. superbum*, magnificent leopard lily, *L. pardalinum*, and variable *L. philadelphicum* arrived in Britain in the eighteenth and nineteenth centuries.

Collectors also had the plants of the Far East under their hot gaze, but the borders of China and Japan remained steadfastly closed against the influences and depredations of the dissolute West until, towards the end of the eighteenth century, some plants started to emerge – legitimately or otherwise.

The pioneering plant hunters of the nineteenth century have become famous in botanical circles. William Kerr sent tiger lilies, *L. lancifolium*, to the Royal Botanic Gardens, Kew; Augustine Henry sent the orange flowers that would become *L. henryi* (see page 152) to an associate. *L. longiflorum* (see page 80) was spotted by Carl Peter Thunberg, and *Lilium speciosum* collected by Philipp Franz von Siebold. And when John Gould Veitch found *L. auratum* (see page 97), around 1862, there was a race to introduce it. Dubbed the "Queen of the Lilies," its looks, poise and fragrance served only to accelerate the prevalent passion for lilies.

The twentieth century dawned adventurously, with the hair-raising discovery of *Lilium regale* by Ernest "Chinese" Wilson nearly costing him his life (see page 179). And, nearly fifty years later, the immensely colorful Frank Kingdon-Ward and his wife Jean, née Macklin, stumbled across *L. mackliniae* atop a mountain in Northern India.

Lilies: the next generation

The Victorian passion for botany is legendary. Daring chaps dashed around the globe and new species poured into gardens to the delight and amazement of all who beheld them.

But gather plants together and, sooner or later, hybrids will emerge; sometimes naturally but often as a result of an irrepressible human desire to improve on nature. While fabulous, lilies had gained a reputation for being challenging and capricious to cultivate. They were exciting; they were expensive; and they were quite likely to die on you after a couple of years. Inevitably, they attracted a certain type of well-heeled horticultural brinksmanship, right up until amenable *Lilium regale* emerged, bringing down both prices and the level of skill required to cultivate this most desirable of flowers.

The backroom boys of experimental horticulture were already on the case, however, and as early as 1869, Francis Parkman, a hobby horticulturist in Boston, had successfully crossed *L. auratum* and *L. speciosum*. Other hybrids followed, including the notable Bellingham Hybrids in the 1920s. Progress accelerated and by the Second World War the hunt for better, brighter, more glamorous and, crucially, more reliable flowers was well underway.

The man who really kick-started the lily revolution was Jan de Graaff. In the late 1930s he gathered the best forms of the species and the available hybrids of the time and began a large-scale program of hybridization at his nursery, Oregon Bulb Farms. In 1941 he struck gold with 'Enchantment', a variety that is still with us today. The legions of plants that followed were a revelation: a reliable, spectacular and versatile legacy that has been taking the world by storm ever since.

On his death in 1989, de Graaff's obituaries summed up his achievements by quoting an article in *Horticulture*. "By dint of rigorous mass hybridization, de Graaff managed to ruin the lily's reputation as an impossible, unobliging garden aristocrat and made of the lily a good, easy-growing garden plant."

Lilies today

The history and genealogy of hybrid lilies is almost biblically complex. The early breeders took the available species plants as their starting point. But, in the 1950s, breeding accelerated dramatically and breakthroughs, spurts of progress and myriad new strains came thick and fast. To make sense of the emerging picture, the Royal Horticultural Society and, in 1963, the North American Lily Society established a system of nine divisions that is now accepted worldwide.

LILY HYBRIDIZATION

Lilies are more likely to interbreed and produce viable offspring if the parents are closely related. So, for example, you are more likely to successfully hybridize two North American species than a North American Lily with one from East Asia.

There may be a number of reasons why this does not work – the gametes (pollen and ovules) may lack fertility; there may be a disparity in chromosome numbers between the parents – lilies are usually diploid, with twenty-four chromosomes arranged in twelve pairs, but they can also be triploid (thirty-six chromosomes) or tetraploid (forty-eight). Or it may be a mechanical issue, such as the pollen grain being unable to travel more than a certain distance down the style towards the ovary.

Hybrids are often more vigorous than their parents. Disease resistance and longevity can be bred in by selecting these characteristics in the seed or pollen parent; it is also possible to select for color and other physical attributes in this way.

Modern hybrids have been bred for robust garden performance, and they are all clones – they all look the same and behave in the same way. Species and wild forms usually reproduce by seed, at least some of the time, and this introduces natural variation. Individuals may not be long-lived and, in the wild, replacement seedlings and small bulbs continuously appear.

The situation has not become any less complex since. Many thousands of varieties have so far been listed in the International Lily Register and there are many more unregistered. Cultivars rise and fall in popularity and new plants appear on the market every year.

The hardy and disease-free Asiatic hybrids, Jan de Graaff's great triumph, became a focus of hybridization around the world and remain a great commercial success. For a while, disease-free Oriental hybrids remained a holy grail; but in the mid-twentieth century Australia and New Zealand led the world, and the work of these Antipodean breeders provided breeding stock for hardier cultivars. These, in turn, were followed by the legendary 'Star Gazer' (see page 115), a breakthrough from grower Leslie Woodriff.

The early cultivars relied on hybridization between interfertile individuals but, legion as these couplings were, natural barriers inhibit breeding between certain species (see page 23). Recently this has been substantially overcome through chemical treatments and embryo culture, resulting in new hybrids such as the much-lauded Orienpets, with their big flowers and light scent, which are the offspring of otherwise incompatible Orientals and Trumpets.

Scent

For millennia, lilies have been prized for their fragrance; for pleasure, for seduction and as a tool for masking unpleasant odors. But while some varieties carry their pleasing perfume as part of a considerable pantheon of charms, others wield their powerful pong like an olfactory offensive weapon.

Scent is a highly subjective thing, and what delights one lily lover can prove overpowering for another. A little fragrance can go a long way, and lily odor in excess has been reported to cause nausea and headaches: that fabulously intoxicating aroma that fills a room can also grab the unsuspecting visitor by the throat.

In lilies, one must look at the ultimate parentage to deduce aromatic firepower. Some species lilies are not particularly fragrant, but *Lilium candidum* and *L. regale* pack a real punch, as do the less well-known *L. erratum, L. tsingtauense* and *L. nepalense*. *Lilium speciosum* is lightly fragrant, while martagon lilies can divide opinion with a light, musky fragrance, perceived variably as pleasant or revolting.

But there is something for everyone. For the sensitive of nose, Asiatic and *Longiflorum* × Asiatic hybrids have little or no scent, and nor do varieties such as *L. pardalinum* and *L. henryi*, while the Orienpets and Easter lilies are pleasant and delicate. If you prefer to pump up the volume, however, *L. candidum* exudes a rich, powerful perfume, as do the potently spicy, somewhat sickly, Oriental hybrids.

Anatomy of a lily

True lilies, *Lilium*, are in the family *Liliaceae*, which encompasses a huge range of other plants, including closely related genera such as *Fritillaria, Cardiocrinum* and *Nomocharis*. Native to the northern hemisphere, lilies range from tiny alpine plants such as *L. nanum*, rarely found in cultivation, to *L. superbum* from the moist meadows of the Americas and *L. candidum*, native to the baking eastern Mediterranean.

Regardless of origin, the flowering stems emerge from an underground bulb; this stores the plant's energy reserves and is made up of loose scales attached at the base. These may be concentric or rhizomatous. Most European and Asiatic species have concentric bulbs, and new bulbs develop within the scales of the parent. *Lilium wilsonii* and *L. nepalense* are exceptions, developing a stoloniferous stem that travels some way underground before it develops new bulblets.

Rhizomatous bulbs are found more often in American species such as *L. canadense* and *L. superbum*. Here, the scaly parent bulb develops a horizontal branch, on the end of which a new bulb develops. As the process repeats, substantial colonies may form. A variation is found in *L. pardalinum*, which forms large clumps atop a beefy, perennial rootstock.

Lily leaves are typically pointed and modest in size. These can be arranged alternately, in whorls or, in some cases, scattered along the stem. The leaves diminish in size the farther away they get from the bulb.

SCATTERED LEAF
ARRANGEMENT

WHORLED LEAF
ARRANGEMENT

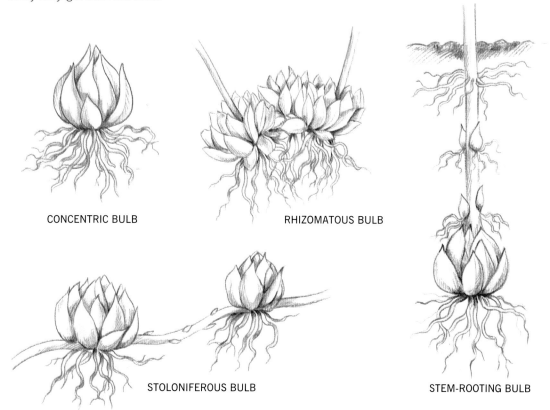

CONCENTRIC BULB

RHIZOMATOUS BULB

STEM-ROOTING BULB

STOLONIFEROUS BULB

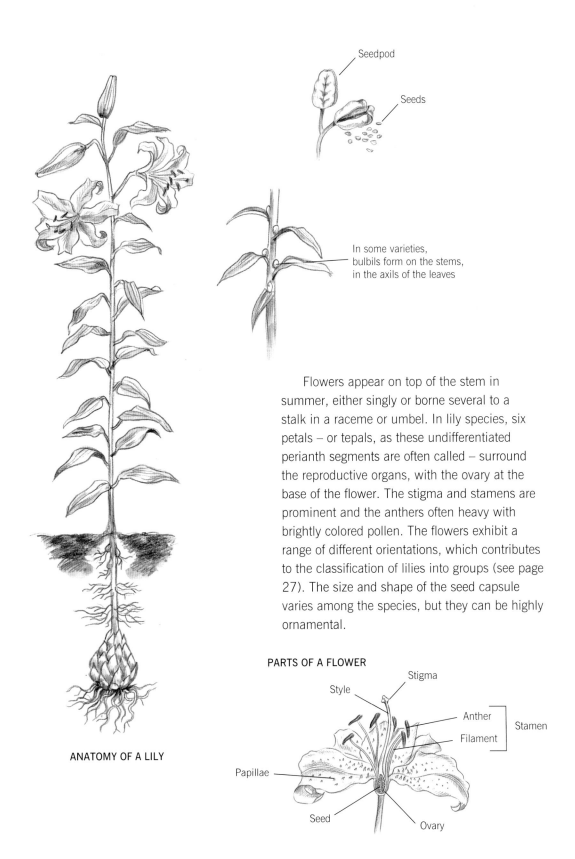

Seedpod

Seeds

In some varieties,
bulbils form on the stems,
in the axils of the leaves

Flowers appear on top of the stem in summer, either singly or borne several to a stalk in a raceme or umbel. In lily species, six petals – or tepals, as these undifferentiated perianth segments are often called – surround the reproductive organs, with the ovary at the base of the flower. The stigma and stamens are prominent and the anthers often heavy with brightly colored pollen. The flowers exhibit a range of different orientations, which contributes to the classification of lilies into groups (see page 27). The size and shape of the seed capsule varies among the species, but they can be highly ornamental.

ANATOMY OF A LILY

PARTS OF A FLOWER

Style

Stigma

Anther

Stamen

Filament

Papillae

Seed

Ovary

Classification and divisions

The classification of lilies is, not to put too fine a point on it, a bit of a headache. Generally speaking, they are placed in one of nine divisions depending on their parentage, then assigned a series of letters that are designed to indicate the shape and habit of the flowers.

The purpose of this is to give gardeners a crib sheet to indicate how each plant will behave: whether it is scented or not, whether it needs acid soil or is lime-tolerant, and whether it is stem-rooting. This information can then inform its care.

Division 1: Early-flowering Asiatic hybrids. These flowers are carried in umbels and are rarely scented.

Division 2: Hybrid lilies, with one parent being either *Lilium martagon* or *L. hansonii*. These have Turk's cap flowers and are sometimes scented.

Division 3: Hybrid lilies that have been bred from European species including *L. candidum* and *L. chalcedonicum*. They often have Turk's cap flowers and can be scented.

Division 4: Hybrid lilies of American parentage, the flowers are most often Turk's caps, but can be funnel-shaped, and they are occasionally scented.

Division 5: Hybrid lilies that are bred from *L. formosanum* and *L. longiflorum*. The large flowers are trumpet- or funnel-shaped and they are often sweetly scented.

TOXICITY IN ANIMALS

Lilies and pets are not a good combination. Although the bulbs can be eaten by humans, and wild rabbits can nibble them unscathed, all parts of a lily are poisonous to cats. Dogs are less affected by lilies, but whatever you grow it is worth being aware of the potential risks to domestic animals.

Ingesting even a small quantity of lily material can cause complete kidney failure in cats. They may eat the leaves but the flowers are particularly toxic, and even licking the pollen off their fur can cause serious poisoning. This is a particular issue when lilies are grown as indoor plants or are introduced as part of a bouquet. In a larger garden, with plenty of room for both pets and plants, lovers of lilies and cats may cut or prop up any flopping flowers to stop the pollen getting on the animals' fur – depending on their individual attitude to risk.

Symptoms of lily poisoning include vomiting, which may include bits of the plants, and signs of kidney failure, such as lethargy, disinterest in food and not passing urine. If you know, or suspect, that your cat has come into contact with lilies, do not delay and take it to the vet immediately.

OUTWARD-FACING FLOWER

UPWARD-FACING FLOWER

TRUMPET

TURK'S CAP

Division 6: Hybrid trumpet lilies derived from Asiatic species, including *L. henryi* and *L. regale*. The flowers are scented, more often than not, and the forms are diverse – trumpets, bowls, with recurved petals or almost flat.

Division 7: Oriental hybrids that have been bred from Far Eastern species – *L. auratum*, *L. japonicum*, *L. rubellum* and *L. speciosum* – those that are not the parents of Division 6 lilies. Usually sweetly scented, the flowers are varied and can be trumpet-shaped, bowl-shaped, recurved or flat.

Division 8: All the lilies that don't fit into one of the other categories.

Division 9: Species lilies, including their forms and varieties.

The letters indicating the habit are arranged as x/y. The first letter indicates how the flower is orientated, so:

a/ upward-facing flowers
b/ outward-facing flowers
c/ downward-facing flowers

The second letter indicates the shape of the flower, so:

/a trumpet-shaped flowers
/b bowl-shaped flowers
/c flat flowers
/d recurved flowers

Therefore, handsome *L. henryi* would be 9 c/d – a species plant with downward-facing flowers and recurved petals.

The problem with this, of course, is the huge amount of interbreeding. Even when parentage is clear, shape and form may be less so and many lovely modern flowers will shrug in the face of these conventions. As a result, the division number is sometimes succeeded by half a dozen letters, as people try to describe them as they are.

For the passionate enthusiast, tweaking and interrogating the nomenclature can while away many a happy afternoon. But for most of us, growing lilies is about pleasure and it is probably best not to get too hung up on classification.

Designing with lilies

In the garden, lilies are supremely versatile. Their ability to slot into their surroundings is unparalleled and their variety limitless: spectacular specimens or team players; a bold, herbaceous border staple; weaving subtly through dappled shade or displayed to perfection against a tastefully painted wall or fence. Small gardens, large gardens, alpine beds or landscapes: there is a lily for them all.

With the exception of *Lilium candidum*, which likes a good baking, the rule of thumb is that lilies like moisture in summer and good drainage in winter, and they hate to be waterlogged. Some are fussier than others about soil pH (see page 205 for more information), but once you have got the measure of your garden and the lilies that you want to grow, just experiment.

In cottage-style gardens, lilies are glorious when combined with roses and sweet peas, clematis and honeysuckle. In the border they complement the other colorful herbaceous plants, and they can play a part in tropical schemes as well. Planting taller varieties into a mixed or shrub border is often successful as the twiggy stems support the lily flowers and provide ongoing interest.

In naturalistic gardens, the elegant Turk's caps excel. Weave martagon lilies or *L. henryi* into light woodland for an exquisite early summer tableau, or scatter *L. pyrenaicum*, *L. hansonii* or *L. pardalinum* into a cultivated meadow to make themselves at home. If they are happy, they may spread to spectacular effect.

DEALING WITH POLLEN STAINING

Lily pollen can stain fabrics, but trying to wash it off will only make things worse. The trick is to brush off any loose pollen, then put the item out in the sunshine – on no account get it wet. In a few hours the sunlight will have bleached the stain and it will be as if it never was.

Oriental lilies hate lime, but on acid soil add them to your ericaceous toolkit, teamed with heathers and azaleas or planted under shrubs and small trees such as *Enkianthus* or *Eucryphia*. In the wild, these lilies are often found in remote, craggy mountains, or pockets of humus among coastal rocks. The smaller and airier varieties can add an unexpected twist to a rock garden, or fill a summer gap in a large alpine trough.

LILIES IN POTS

Pots packed with juicy lilies look fantastic on the terrace and add the wow factor to even the smallest courtyard garden. It is also the perfect way to grow the bulbs even if your soil conditions or pH are not conducive to lilies, but ensure that the pot has drainage holes and take care not to overwater (see page 212).

The more compact varieties can also be used as house plants. Just bring them inside and put them in a cool, bright location, out of full sun – bearing in mind the usual cautions regarding pets (see page 27) and the risk of pollen staining. An attractive sleeve pot or simple saucer will help to protect surfaces and furniture.

If you are a keen gardener with packed borders, a neat trick is to plant your lily bulbs into pots in autumn, with a little slow-release fertilizer to keep them going, and then plant them out where you want them in spring.

AS A CUT FLOWER

Whether as a single variety, combined strategically for color and form, or in a mixed posy, lilies make wonderful cut flowers. In recent decades, the upward-facing Asiatic hybrids have become popular with florists, primarily because their shape makes them easy to pack and transport. But grown at home no such strictures apply, and a vase of statuesque Madonna lilies or airy, architectural Turk's caps can be both spectacular and unexpected.

A bunch of matching lilies is simple and striking, while a single stem in a heavy-bottomed vase makes a bold statement. Alternatively, surround them with congenial greenery and flattering associates, such as roses and asparagus fern; foxgloves, *Alchemilla* and ivy; or gerbera and chrysanthemums to provide an extra hit of color. If pollen staining is likely to be a problem, remove the anthers with a small pair of scissors.

If you are harvesting from your perennial border, make sure that you leave enough of the stem and leaves to feed the bulb and allow it to bulk up and flower again next year. And if you want to pick a lot, consider creating a dedicated cutting patch, where the hard-working bulbs can either be fed and cosseted, or replaced annually.

CUTTING LILIES

The best time to cut lilies is just as the first bud starts to open; the rest will open in sequence over the next few days. Putting the flowers straight into a bucket of clean water minimizes wilting.

Remember to remove the leaves from the lower part of the stem, and it helps to refresh the water in the vase occasionally, trimming the stem as you do so. In hot weather, a tiny drop of bleach or white vinegar mixed into the water will slow bacterial growth and help to make the flowers last longer; treated well and kept in cool conditions, they can last up to two weeks.

Societies and organizations

America
North American Lily Society: This group has members in almost every state and contacts around the world. There are several affiliated regional lily societies in the US and Canada.
www.lilies.org

UK
Royal Horticultural Society (RHS) Lily Group: Aims to promote understanding of lilies, and their growing and conservation.
www.rhslilygroup.org

Europe
Danish Iris and Lily Club: Promotes knowledge of plants of the class Liliopsida, including the genera Iridaceae, Liliaceae, Hemerocallidaceae and others.
www.dils.dk

The European Lily Society: Membership organization providing experts and enthusiasts with a newsletter, lily exhibition and seed list.
www.liliengesellschaft.org

The Czech Lily Society: An association that aims to bring together lilies and those who love them and want to grow them.
http://martagon-lilie.cz

The Antipodes
The New Zealand Lily Society: Community of like-minded enthusiasts helping people learn and discover the magic of lilies.
www.lovelilies.nz

The South Australian Lilium and Bulb Society Inc.: Provides expert advice and tips to lily gardeners.
https://liliumbulb.org.au

Auckland Lily Society: A group that shares tips and advice on growing lilies.
https://www.facebook.com/AucklandLilySociety/

North-West Tasmanian Lilium Society Inc.: A small group based on the North-West Coast of Tasmania that aims to encourage, inform and assist those interested in the genus *Lilium*.
liliestasmania.com.au.camlilies.com.au

Elegant
and Dainty

Soft Music

Soft Music is the perfect flower for lovers of luxury. Everything about it implies elegance and eschews the notion of hard graft. The pink and yellow tones that infuse rather than stain the white bloom; the gentle curves of the flower. The tiny freckles a delicate pointillism around the central nub of as-yet-unopened petals.

This is a flower that is almost decadent, practically sybaritic, but undoubtedly special. It nestles into a bride's bouquet or boudoir as if it belongs there; it would welcome in new motherhood and speaks volumes on behalf of an adoring lover, to one who might be cherished and nurtured.

Long-lasting, pollen-free and achingly lovely, it is the flower to inspire self-care and make the world around it a little more beautiful, and a little more fragrant; filled with wine, love, flowers and all manner of pretty things to enjoy.

....

Lilium 'Soft Music'
Flower type Bowl-shaped, double blooms
Division 7
Average height 3–5 ft
Flower size Large
Color White with yellow tones and pale pink edging
Flowering time July onwards
Scent Delicately perfumed
Soil type Rich and lime-free
In the garden Lovely in containers on a stylish summery terrace
As a cut flower Luxurious and desirable, a wonderful table centerpiece

Ariadne

It is hard to beat the sophistication of Turk's cap lilies, and Ariadne is a classic. Tiny, dainty, peach-pink baubles are suspended airily around a tall stem, like an expensive filigree Christmas tree or a living candelabra.

Known as the North hybrids, Ariadne, like Eros, is one of the Asiatic hybrid lilies bred by Dr Chris North, who was based in Scotland and did a considerable amount of work culturing lily embryos on agar plates. In this case, he used genetic material from *Lilium lankongense* and *L. davidii*, the latter of which has been shown to confer virus tolerance on its offspring.

In classical myth, Ariadne is the daughter of King Minos, who fell in love with Theseus. She helped him in his quest to slay the Minotaur by giving him a thread to pay out as he entered the dread maze, and which he could follow back to escape. It is tempting to draw parallels with other feisty ladies of yore and their associations with lilies; however, since Dr North's Greek Gods series of lilies also includes Euridice, Adonis, Theseus and Pan, it seems more likely that he just liked the idea of the evocatively high-powered names for his choice plant selections.

....

Lilium 'Ariadne'
Flower type Turk's cap
Division 1
Average height 4–6 ft
Flower size Small
Color Pale, dusty rose
Flowering time Midsummer
Scent Light
Soil type Any good garden soil
In the garden Wonderful at the back of the border and a good statement plant set against a foil of dark foliage or a contrasting painted surface
As a cut flower Beautiful, but you need a tall vase to accommodate the soaring flower spike

Salmon Star

Naming new plants is a game of two halves. There are those who name their plants after something important, such as classical gods or beloved relatives. There was also the eminent and idiosyncratic horticulturist and breeder, Isabella Preston (1881–1965), who named her lilies after the Allied planes deployed in the Second World War (the Fighter Aircraft Series) and the secretaries that worked alongside her at the Central Experimental Farm in Ottawa (the Stenographer Series). And then there are those that look at the plant and speak as they find.

Examples of the second type are numerous: the snowdrop called 'Grumpy', the apple 'Leathercoat Russet' and the Hydrangea 'Glam Rock'. And when it came to this lily, you can imagine the breeder looking hard at his or her new creation, observing the orange-pink star motif in the middle of the flower and thinking "Brilliant, 'Salmon Star', that'll do!"

Fortunately, there is nothing fishy about this flower. It is open and elegantly shaped, gazing upwards towards the sky. The white petals are washed with pale salmon and apricot, which is tempered with deeper, pink-red spots and bold ginger pollen on the anthers.

Possibly best of all, its genuinely dwarf habit means that it is ideal for small spaces, never needs staking and excels in sunny containers.

....

Lilium 'Salmon Star'
Flower type Upward- and outward-facing bowl
Division 7
Average height 16–30 in
Flower size Very large
Color White, apricot and salmon-pink
Flowering time Late summer
Scent Very fragrant
Soil type Ericaceous and free-draining
In the garden A dwarf plant that is perfect for raised beds and containers
As a cut flower Beautiful and unusual

Natalia

Soft, luscious and pollen-free, Natalia is a good-tempered sort of flower and acts as a fine advert for the Roselily® Series of Oriental hybrids.

The crisply concave and rather pointed petals are pertly layered, while the margins are ruffled and frilled. The soft fragrance does not overpower when the flowers are brought indoors, while the double-raspberry-ripple effect combines well, both in a bouquet and in a border.

In the garden, the plant is relatively compact, ideal for the front of a planting scheme, in sun or part shade, and you should be able to do without staking.

More than capable of holding its own without company, floriferous Natalia also plays reliably nicely with other plants and it looks great in a pot, where it will pep up a late-summer patio alongside dahlias, salvias and seasonal bedding.

....

Lilium Roselily Natalia®
Flower type Upward-facing, bowl-shaped double bloom
Division 7
Average height 28–36 in
Flower size Large
Color Pink
Flowering time Mid- to late summer
Scent Prettily fragrant
Soil type Free-draining and rather acid
In the garden Compact and stocky enough for the front of the border, or good in matching pots on either side of a door to create a frame
As a cut flower Illuminates a room

Lilium leichtlinii

It was sheer happenstance that brought *Lilium leichtlinii* into cultivation. Unknown and unanticipated, it was discovered as an interloper in a shipment of *L. auratum* that was received by the Veitch nursery in the south-west of England in the late nineteenth century, but horticulturists being horticulturists, they grew it on and kept it.

Lilium leichtlinii is delightful, with its brilliant lemon-yellow petals moderated by a liberal freckling of sable, and anthers to match; it is quiet rather than ostentatious. The impression is striped and spotted, feline even – although more tabby cat than tiger.

Native to Japan, this lily is found in mountains and moist areas, often among grasses, and particularly on and near Mount Yatsugatake, in central Honshū. The yellow-flowered "type" of the species was named for German botanist Max Leichtlin, yet there is a far more common variety, the orange-flowered *L. leichtlinii var. maximowiczii*. Found all over Japan and even reported in Vladivostok and elsewhere, it could be argued that this should really be the species rather than the variety, and the real surprise is not so much that the lily arrived by accident as that it was the yellow one, the rarer of its kind.

As a result, *L. leichtlinii* is not all that common in cultivation either, but it does exist if you know where to look. The stoloniferous, stem-rooting bulb produces an erect spike and around half a dozen flowers are borne daintily on the end of long, strong flower stalks.

It needs an acid soil and should be planted in a semi-shaded position with as much leaf mold as you can muster. It will form good-sized clumps when happy.

....

Lilium leichtlinii
Flower type Pendant flower with reflexed petals
Division 9
Average height Variable, 3–4½ ft
Flower size Small
Color Brilliant lemon-yellow with maroon freckles
Flowering time Midsummer
Scent Unscented
Soil type Acid soil with plenty of organic matter
In the garden A beautiful subject for a naturalistic garden, teamed with airy grasses and soft, romantic flowers
As a cut flower Very sophisticated in a vase

Polar Star

Some plants thoroughly deserve their popularity, and Polar Star is blessed with the sort of classic good looks and innate fabulousness that is guaranteed to turn heads.

The color scheme is an adaptable blend of pistachio and ivory, the flowers are large and lavish and their pollen-free ways won't make a mess of dresses or décor. The long, crimped petals are loosely curled and sweetly fragrant; formal, yet at the same time, blown and blousy.

The only thing that slightly jars is the name – and that feels a bit like nit-picking – but the shape is less that of a star than a loose but rather attractive feather duster. It lacks the icy whiteness of the pole star, twinkling in the night sky, and if it references the polar star, *per se*, surely the definite article is essential?

Yet there are polar qualities to this lily, after a fashion. The blueish, greenish quality evokes light shining through icebergs and sea caves, powerful and eldritch. The not-quite-white of a polar bear prowling across the snow, its transparent fur cleverly trapping the light and bouncing it around to camouflage the beast in its environment.

Nature is a wonderful thing, and maybe it does not do to ask why. Maybe Polar Star is simply a delightful, abundant, double Oriental lily. Wonderful at weddings and fitting at funerals, it is welcome everywhere it goes.

....

Lilium 'Polar Star'
Flower type Upward- and outward-facing and fully double
Division 7
Average height 28–39 in
Flower size Large to very large
Color White
Flowering time Late summer and even into early autumn
Scent Exceptionally delicious
Soil type Moist, well-drained and lime-free
In the garden A striking addition to a white garden, with other seasonal white flowers such as phlox, late roses, asters and gray or glaucous foliage
As a cut flower Fresh and cheerful, these lilies excel in a vase, displaying not a jot of funereal gloom

Guinea Gold

This peerless hybrid lily is a simply beautiful garden plant. Loose towers of dappled flowers are suspended from the main stem like a delicate golden jingle of bells; buds opening in a slow-motion ripple, running up a stem that is sparsely scattered with pale green foliage.

The flowers themselves are good enough to eat; the golden-bronze tones of a brandy-snap basket filled with crème Chantilly and a splash of blackcurrant sauce. Speckled with cinnamon and edged with gold leaf, it is the ultimate in glamour and luxury.

In the garden, Guinea Gold is a reliable plant that should increase well, although it may take its time. It looks glorious in a woodland-edge setting, but it will take sunshine or part shade, and it looks particularly delightful when it is placed to catch the rays of the setting sun.

....

Lilium x *dalhansonii* 'Guinea Gold'
Flower type Turk's cap
Division *2*
Average height 3½–4½ ft
Flower size Small
Color Old gold with undertones of bronze
Flowering time Early to midsummer
Scent Light and musky
Soil type Any good, free-draining garden soil
In the garden Perfect in a classic cottage-garden border
As a cut flower Elegant and really rather sophisticated

Sorbonne

This fabulous, floriferous and fragrant Oriental lily is the exact color of any number of tempting childhood sweets; sugar mice and marshmallows, sugared almonds and shrimps. Its demeanor is irresistibly evocative of sunshine, roses and other, older lilies, sending us back in time to grandmother's cottage garden, restored and flowering among us once again.

It is not a shy and retiring flower by any means. Each bloom is enormous – big and bold; the inherent sweetness tempered by a magenta streak down the center of each petal and the intense crimson freckles around and upon the scattered papillae.

The name Sorbonne reeks of class and sophistication, too. The Sorbonne has been a part of the University of Paris since it was set up in the thirteenth century. As a building and a college, as well as an area, it has been through many iterations and reiterations in its role as a center of intelligence, research and culture, and has recently become a university in its own right. One notable nineteenth-century alumna was radiation scientist Marie Curie.

....

Lilium 'Sorbonne'
Flower type Open and upward-facing
Division 7
Average height 3–5 ft
Flower size Very large
Color Pink and lavender
Flowering time Mid- to late summer
Scent Lightly fragrant
Soil type The acidic side of neutral
In the garden Lovely along a shady boundary where the fresh, light flowers will stand out and add a splash of color
As a cut flower Classically good-looking

Lilium canadense var. coccineum
syn. American Meadow Lily

A native of eastern North America, *Lilium canadense* is widely distributed from Quebec to Pennsylvania and Alabama, although it is far from common. It has the distinction of being the first American lily species to arrive on European shores, and while it is choice indeed, it is not always that easy to grow.

Its natural preference is for damp woodland near a stream, with plenty of moisture for the roots even in the hottest summer, yet well-drained enough that the bulb does not rot. Fully hardy, it shrugs in the face of winter snow. In the garden, it is best to give it deep, acid soil with plenty of leaf mold, and which never dries out.

While it may not be entirely biddable, this plant is supremely lovely. The stems are erect and fringed with regular whorls of green leaves.

The well-spaced flowers are pendent bells, an elegant array resembling a particularly gorgeous and well-designed art deco lampshade.

Natural populations vary somewhat in coloring, but the cultivated form of *L. canadense* is usually clear yellow with fine spots airbrushed into the center, while the red form, *L. canadense* var. *coccineum*, is also delightful. It too faces demurely downwards and has petals that flare rather than reflex. The petal color is rich, rubied and complex, deepening to blue-purple slate where it adjoins the stem.

....

Lilium canadense var. *coccineum*
Flower type Downward-facing bell
Division 9
Average height Variable, around 3 ft
Flower size Small
Color Gorgeous rich red
Flowering time High summer
Scent Unscented
Soil type Moist and acidic, with lashings of humus
In the garden Wonderful in a woodland garden alongside ericaceous shrubs; it is stoloniferous so it is not a good container subject
As a cut flower Exquisite, but almost too beautiful to cut

Corsage

Corsage is a lily with connections. Bred at Oregon Bulb Farms by that titan among lily men, Jan de Graaff, it is one of the seedlings produced from an original cross between Edith Cecilia and Lemon Queen. This produced a group of Asiatic hybrid lilies that became known as the Harlequin Hybrids, due to their spectacular range of colors.

Although many of her contemporaries have faded away, Corsage, first registered In 1961, is still going strong and to this day it is loved and appreciated in gardens across the globe.

In addition to breeding and stamina, Corsage has other winning qualities. The outward-facing flowers are a pleasing deep rose at the tips, fading through pale pink to cream at the center, and freckled with a juicy raspberry crush.

The prominent, upward-facing style is similarly pink-tipped, but the flower is pollen-free and the rudimentary anthers are subtly creamy.

Like other Asiatics, Corsage dislikes acid conditions, so if you are not on limestone or at least neutral soil, it is best grown in a container.

....

Lilium 'Corsage'
Flower type Outward-facing, flattish bowl
Division 1
Average height Around 3–4 ft
Flower size Small
Color Raspberries and cream
Flowering time Early to midsummer
Scent Unscented
Soil type Free-draining, neutral or alkaline
In the garden Charming and subtle with classic good looks, Corsage fits seamlessly into most planting schemes
As a cut flower Elegance personified and pollen-free to boot

Helvetia

The personification of Switzerland, Helvetia is often depicted as a stately female figure in the classical style. With her hair in plaits around her head, she is draped in classical robes and clasps a spear and shield – similar in attire to Britannia, but with a laurel wreath rather than a helmet.

Yet despite the classical representation, the name actually comes from a Celtic tribe, the Helvetii, who were based around the Swiss plateau prior to the domination of Rome, and the allegory in its current form has coalesced gradually, from several others, over a period of some 300 years.

As might be expected, this poetic embodiment of a nation in floral form is stately and proud. Her petals are ruffled at the edges and curl crisply at the tips, the pure white touched with the merest hint of green at the nectaries, on the stamens and along the midrib.

Planted into black or charcoal-colored containers, Helvetia by herself will make a fragrant statement in a formal setting, or could be combined with other white and pink flowers for an additional shot of prettiness.

....

Lilium 'Helvetia'
Flower type Upward-facing with reflexed petals
Division 7
Average height 3–4 ft
Flower size Very large
Color White
Flowering time Mid- to late summer
Scent Highly fragrant
Soil type Does best in an acidic substrate
In the garden Lovely near the front of the border and in containers
As a cut flower Wonderful as part of a cascade of blooms at a wedding

Claude Shride

Martagon lilies are native to Europe, and since its introduction at some point prior to 1980, Claude Shride has become something of a modern classic.

In the garden it is bold yet elegant, producing racemes of small flowers that each resembles an open, damson-colored globe. But closer inspection reveals that the heart of the flower is touched with golden brushstrokes and stippled with mahogany, while the prominent stamens are a similar shade of gold.

While Claude Shride may sulk for a year or so before flowering, it bulks up nicely with time to create loose spires of blooms that hang, settle and quiver like a cloud of exotic butterflies.

Plant in a sheltered, partly shaded position in rich, well-drained soil that is ideally neutral to alkaline.

....

Lilium martagon 'Claude Shride'
Flower type Downward-facing with recurved petals in the Turk's cap style
Division 2
Average height 3–6 ft
Flower size Small
Color Deep crimson with a splash of tangerine
Flowering time Early summer
Scent Fragrant, fresh, citrus aroma
Soil type Free-draining; easy-going, but prefers neutral to alkaline soil
In the garden Looks good with acid-green euphorbias and purple alliums
As a cut flower Very good; use to anchor orange or pink companions

Albufeira

Memories and impressions stay with us and it does not take much time spent with beautiful, evocative Albufeira before one sinks into a rather blissful reverie.

The blooms are scented and of magnificent size, but it is its pink-and-white prettiness and the implications of the name that grab you most.

The original Albufeira is a small town in Portugal, located on the southern coast of mainland Europe. The sea and the sky are brilliant blue and the old town is famed for its white and pastel buildings. As the sun sinks in the sky, the pink sunset intensifies the candy shades making them richer and rosier, the perfect backdrop for a stroll on the warm sand or an iced drink *al fresco* – building memories you want to keep.

Robust in the garden and pretty in a vase, this *Longiflorum* × Asiatic hybrid is an echo of idealized Mediterranean loveliness that will transport those of us in significantly cooler climates to a much-needed holiday paradise.

....

Lilium 'Albufeira'
Flower type Upward-facing open bowl
Division 8
Average height 4 ft
Flower size Large
Color A sugary pink and white
Flowering time Early to midsummer
Scent Light fragrance
Soil type Any reasonable garden soil
In the garden Lovely in a border and the color pops when planted in front of plummy *Cotinus* 'Grace' or inky *Sambucus nigra*
As a cut flower Striking and classically good-looking

Lilium candidum syn. Madonna Lily

Quite understandably, *Lilium candidum* is a classic; culturally significant for millennia (see page 17) its extensive spread has been facilitated through human religious and empire-building excursions. As a result, it is now extensively naturalized in suitable habitats across southern and eastern Europe, and its true origin is uncertain, although it is thought to hail from the Caucasus or parts of the Middle East.

The specific epithet "candidum," as applied by Linnaeus, means "shining white," yet the plant is also known as the Annunciation lily, Ascension lily, Bourbon lily, French lily, Juno's rose and St Joseph's lily. Although the flower spikes can positively bristle with buds – up to twenty on an established plant – only a few blooms will be open at any one time.

In the garden, *L. candidum* is a little bit of an anomaly. Lilies tend to prefer a little shade and some moisture, but Madonna lilies like to be baked in bright, hot sun and they do well on sharply draining alkaline soil, where they should be planted shallowly, about 1 inch deep. They are also less hardy than some. Uniquely, in late summer the bulbs produce rosettes of leaves which will overwinter, and flower the following summer.

If this paragon has a fault, it is that it is susceptible to the rot caused by fungal infection *Botrytis*. If you don't want to use fungicides, try growing it away from other lilies. Taller specimens should be staked.

....

Lilium candidum
Flower type Open trumpet
Division 9
Average height 4–6 ft
Flower size Medium
Color Freshest white
Flowering time High summer
Scent Light and sophisticated
Soil type Light, chalky and free-draining
In the garden Back of the border with lush-flowering companions to disguise the leaves that become tatty as the season progresses
As a cut flower Magnificent

Anouska

A compact and floriferous garden plant that is also outstanding in containers, Roselily Anouska® is a flawless and fragrant cut flower that is perfect for celebrations and joyous gatherings.

Delicate and achingly pretty, this particular flower is a double Oriental with wide, pointed petals that are arranged in layers, to create the impression of a bunch of waterlilies in a vase. The color is gorgeous, a clean, almost blue-white with a pink picotee edge, sometimes faint and narrow and sometimes running slightly into the surrounding purity.

Unlike the other Roselilies, Anouska has just a little pollen, but whether this is a problem or not is very much down to individual tastes, and, as a flower, it has much to recommend it.

....

Lilium Roselily Anouska®
Flower type Upward-facing, bowl-shaped double flowers
Division 7
Average height 28–36 in
Flower size Large
Color Blush pink
Flowering time Mid- to late summer
Scent Yes
Soil type Acidic soil or ericaceous compost
In the garden Lovely in containers
As a cut flower The beautiful soft colors are ideal for a wedding, or perhaps to celebrate the arrival of a new baby

Eros

Bred by Dr Chris North and registered in 1977, Eros has stood the test of time and is still going strong. A sterile, triploid, Asiatic hybrid, it has a complex parentage which includes classics such as Citronella and Destiny, both of which were popular in the middle of the twentieth century.

The flowers are beautiful, lightly fragrant and with an understated dusty rose color at the tips that morphs into tangerine at the heart of the bloom, which is also speckled with deepest, darkest chocolate.

Eros flowers in high summer, and the numerous bluish buds, which run up the stem like a long wand of bells, open one after the other. A good and reliable plant, Eros is anecdotally more heat-tolerant than some other lilies. And while it is worth being slightly cautious when putting the name of this particular variety into a search engine, the charm and poise of the flower outweighs any slight, unrelated frisson of iniquity.

....

Lilium 'Eros'
Flower type Turk's cap
Division 1
Average height 3–4½ ft
Flower size Small
Color Plum-coral
Flowering time Midsummer
Scent Lightly fragrant
Soil type Any good garden soil
In the garden Lovely either in the border or planted on the edge of a woodland
As a cut flower Beautiful and dainty

Lilium longiflorum

syn. Easter Lily, Bermuda Lily, Trumpet Lily

Native to a slender slice of East Asia, stretching from Japan to the Philippines, *Lilium longiflorum* is charming, fragrant and decorative. What's more, it punches way above its weight on the floral world stage due to its adoption as the "Easter" lily, a symbol of hope, purity and resurrection in the Christian faith (see page 18).

The large flowers are delightful, with perhaps half a dozen carried atop a stem clad in glossy, dark green leaves. Each long, white trumpet is palest green at the base, fading to white, while the central stigma, stamens and anthers are a faded, buttery hue.

Left to its own devices, *L. longiflorum* and its cultivars would bloom in summer – usually between June and August in much of the northern hemisphere. But to perform at its best at Easter, the bulbs are forced. This is done by keeping the potted bulbs in cool temperatures – they need a period of chill in order to flower – and once they are in growth, the amount of light and warmth they receive is moderated to control bloom time. Unlike many lilies, this species is not fully hardy in cold climates.

When potted Easter lilies have finished flowering, you can plant them out into the garden. Acclimatize the plants gradually to outdoor conditions before removing the pot, loosening the roots and settling them into the soil. The stem-rooting bulbs may take a couple of years to recover, but should flower at the normal time when they are ready. The plants are generally sturdy and don't need staking. Popular cultivars include White

....

Lilium longiflorum
Flower type Outward-facing trumpet
Division 9
Average height 3 ft
Flower size Large to very large
Color Pure white fading to chartreuse at the base of the flower
Flowering time High to late summer
Scent Sweetly delicious
Soil type Likes damp, neutral to acid soil, but will tolerate some lime if it must
In the garden Blends harmoniously with whites and greens; experiment with ferns, *Nicotiana sylvestris* and *Alchemilla mollis* or combine with soft pink phlox and roses
As a cut flower Heaven-sent

Wild
and Wonderful

Magic Star

Bold, flamboyant and striped like a pair of witches' stockings, Magic Star could never be accused of holding back, but it is fun nevertheless.

The flowers of this Oriental lily are fully double, magnificent in size and blessed with a heady and exotic fragrance. The frilled petals have a pale pink base color with a central magenta streak – a little like a sucked stick of seaside rock – and they are gaily spattered with dark alizarin.

Each strong stem brandishes its fistful of ragamuffin blooms erect above the deep-green foliage, so it can hold its own in the garden and it is monstrously cheerful when used to decorate a room.

If you grow azaleas and dwarf rhododendrons, try planting Magic Star nearby, in sun or part shade, to take up the baton once their equally brash flowers have faded. Alternatively, it can be used to provide late-summer interest in the mixed border with *Dahlia* 'Karma Choc', *Eupatorium purpureum* and *Calamagrostis brachytricha*.

....

Lilium 'Magic Star'
Flower type Outward-facing double
Division 7
Average height 28–36 in
Flower size Large to very large
Color Pink, hot pink and white
Flowering time Late summer to early autumn
Scent Beautifully scented
Soil type Rich, moist and acidic
In the garden Makes an eye-catching subject for a patio pot or can be weaved into the border with pink and white daisies and phlox
As a cut flower Bold and characterful

Exotic Sun

Beautiful, fragrant and blessed with flowers that are not simply substantial, but are truly magnificent, Exotic Sun is the joyful hybrid offspring of a Trumpet lily and a double Oriental and combines some of the finest qualities of both.

In truth, there is something ethereal and otherworldly about this particular creature. It is dramatic and glorious, shot through with filigree of light; the long, curling petals resemble a white-hot ball of flames captured by camera or rendered almost static in the view through the window of celestial time.

In the garden and in the vase, Exotic Sun eschews the prosaic, and while it is good teamed with the usual denizens of a hot border, or woven among pale blues and deep greens, when permitted to perform its bewitching intergalactic solo without interruption, it is outstanding.

....

Lilium 'Exotic Sun'
Flower type Double, upward- and outward-facing bowl
Division 8
Average height 4–4¼ ft+
Flower size Very large
Color Soft lemon yellow
Flowering time Midsummer
Scent Yes
Soil type Good, free-draining garden soil, unfussy about pH
In the garden A fabulous feature plant
As a cut flower Exemplary

Saltarello

With up to eight flowers per mighty stem and magnificent in stature, Saltarello is one of the newer, taller varieties often known as tree lilies or skyscraper lilies. Pleasantly fragrant and undoubtedly dramatic, it is a popular Oriental-Trumpet hybrid (Orienpet), which is both gorgeous and prolific.

The petals are long, reflexed and slightly ruffled towards the tips and the colors alone are scrumptious – butterscotch and honey, peach and mango, banana ice cream with toffee sauce. The orangey hue fades a little with age but, whichever way you look at it, Saltarello is melt-in-the-mouth delicious.

The *saltarello* or *saltarelle* in French, was a lively dance that was popular in medieval and Renaissance Italy, and has since become adopted as a folk dance. Fittingly, the eponymous flower skips and leaps to great heights in the border, although it is a bit on the large size for containers.

Lilium 'Saltarello'
Flower type Upward- and outward-facing, bowl-shaped flowers
Division 8
Average height 5–6½ ft
Flower size Large to very large
Color Butterscotch-cream
Flowering time High to late summer
Scent Highly fragrant
Soil type Free-draining, neutral to slightly acidic
In the garden The vivid orange-yellow color works well with summer-flowering perennials such as heleniums and cone flowers
As a cut flower A large lily that needs a large vase, Saltarello will make a statement in a good-sized room

Kuchibeni

When *Lilium auratum* was introduced in the late nineteenth century, the western gardening world went wild. Dubbed "The Queen of Lilies," it is fabulous indeed: the flowers are huge, some of the very biggest there are, and they are produced for weeks over late summer and into autumn. The scent, furthermore, is glorious, powerful enough to knock you off your feet, while giddily transporting you to the heavens.

Native to the Honshū region of Japan, *L. auratum* is found on the edge of mountain woodland where thin humus covers volcanic ash and lava rubble. Known in Japanese as *yama-yuri*, meaning "mountain lily," the epithet *auratum* derives from the Latin word for gold, and refers to the gilded flash of yellow that runs up the center of the raspberry-flecked white petals, and the ornamental tiger-gold of the anthers. It can also be known, more functionally, as the Japanese golden ray lily.

Early cultivators often came unstuck by overfeeding this paragon; too rich a diet can cause disease and early death. So emulate the poor soil and instant drainage of its mountainous home, keep it dry in winter and in summer give it sufficient water and lashings of sunshine and, with luck, the flowers will come.

Due to its many excellent qualities, *L. auratum* has become a parent of many modern Orientals, but the variety Kuchibeni is a form rather than any sort of hybrid, and arose from seed wild-collected in Aizu, which is within the Honshū region. The gorgeous raspberry-cinnamon stripe that surrounds and engulfs the leitmotif gold markings and the stronger wine-colored flecks are dramatic and fabulous: Nature's own improvement on a gilded lily.

....

Lilium auratum var. *platyphyllum* 'Kuchibeni'
Flower type Outward-facing bowl
Division 9
Average height 3–6½ ft
Flower size Very large
Color White with gold and red flashes
Flowering time Mid- to late summer and even into autumn
Scent Very fragrant
Soil type Poor, neutral to acid, free-draining
In the garden A heaven-sent focal point
As a cut flower Absolutely glorious

Distant Drum

Where some lilies are all poise, elegance and sophistication, Distant Drum dances to a different tune.

Facing almost upwards, the long petals are striped and brushed with rose and raspberry; fading to a whiter cream-pink at the margins and with a twist of pistachio at the center. It is almost reminiscent of Star Gazer, but it rocks its double Oriental anarchy with such style as to make that old faithful look sedate.

Distant Drum is a flower that must have supped deeply from the cup of punk culture. You could imagine it hanging out with Andy Warhol, singing along to classic David Bowie and Debbie Harry, chatting to Sid Vicious at a bar for a bet and taking style tips from Toyah Willcox and Vivienne Westwood.

At the same time, Distant Drum is pretty and so fragrant, it even has the grace to be pollen-free; its inherent discord is just an echo, a whisper of iconoclasm, a suggestion of social change. It is a flower for free spirits and dreamers, the proud and the passionate; perfect for statement vases and brides with attitude. Punky, to be sure, but perfectly pretty besides.

Lilium 'Distant Drum'
Flower type Outward-facing double
Division 7
Average height 32–36 in
Flower size Large
Color Pink
Flowering time Mid- to late summer
Scent Fragrant
Soil type Humus-rich and lime-free
In the garden Use informally in the border or plant up large containers
to appreciate its scent and beauty on the deck
As a cut flower Team with pink roses, bronze dahlias and acid-green panicum
grass, and *Alchemilla mollis*, for a pretty summer arrangement

Sunny Azores

This Oriental pot lily is part of the Lily Looks™ range, in which the Sunny Series is (mostly) named after islands, and includes Sunny Bahamas, Sunny Martinique and Sunny Granada.

As its name implies, Sunny Azores is a happy little plant. Naturally short and compact, it is ideal grown in pots or brought inside to perfume a room. In the garden, meanwhile, no staking is required and it will attract pollinators, and even hummingbirds, if you are fortunate enough to have them.

The clear white of the ruffled petals is illuminated by a golden glow at the center of the flower, effortlessly evoking sunlight on white sands and a tropical island paradise. Plant a generous number of bulbs into pots for a spectacular display, or expand the holiday theme with splashes of bright blue and lime green.

....

Lilium 'Sunny Azores'
Flower type Upward- and outward-facing bowl
Division 7
Average height 14–18 in
Flower size Large to very large
Color White with yellow
Flowering time Mid- to late summer
Scent Intoxicating
Soil type Best in acidic soil or ericaceous compost
In the garden A great container variety
As a cut flower Exquisite

Playtime

Oriental lilies tend to be upbeat and extrovert at the best of times, but there are a few that go the extra mile. And when it comes to charisma, drama and arresting good looks, Playtime's magnificent flower is blessed with an almost pantomime quality.

It has, of course, a sweet and delicious scent. Then there is the arms-thrown-wide, striding across the stage, doublet-and-hose habit of the flowers; large, sumptuous, ruffled-and-frilled blooms that are one stop short of being a little too much.

Still funnier and fruitier, our hero comes with just a dash of the Widow Twankies. It has qualities of coloring that are reminiscent of a rather indulgent pudding – the fruit sundae that mixes vanilla ice-cream with raspberry and banana, or lemon-and-lime sorbet with diced watermelon and a decadent splash of chartreuse.

Undoubtedly born to be a star of stage, screen and sitcom, Playtime is at its best holding court in containers and is the decadent darling of florists everywhere.

Lilium 'Playtime'
Flower type Outward-facing bowl
Division 7
Average height 3–4 ft
Flower size Very large
Color White with a yellow and fuchsia-pink stripe
Flowering time Mid- to late summer
Scent Strong fragrance
Soil type Acidic and free-draining
In the garden A real star
As a cut flower Eye-popping

Perfect Joy

Many lilies give the impression of cheerfulness, but there is a particularly gay and enthusiastic quality to Perfect Joy.

The name alone evokes something uncomplicated, pristine and light-hearted, and the flower itself does nothing to dispel this. Borne atop a small plant with sturdy, upright stems, the fat, green buds open into wide stars that smile appealingly upwards. The petals are white with rose-tinted tips, and the center of the flower is stippled and freckled with raspberry-truffle, a color that echoes that of the anthers before the rusty pollen matures.

This small, pink and white collision of color and form seems rather like a flower that was drawn rather than grown, a vegetable embodiment of a particularly cute Japanese cartoon – all candyfloss hair, exaggerated eyes and slightly disturbing sweet expression.

Easy to grow and ideal for pots, Perfect Joy likes a reasonably sheltered spot with plenty of sun, as does Lollipop, which is a similar alternative.

As part of a bouquet to celebrate a christening or baby shower, Perfect Joy is lovely with other pink and white flowers, or you can tone down the overwhelming sugariness with the addition of plums and bronzes, in both the border and in the vase.

....

Lilium 'Perfect Joy'
Flower type Upward-facing bowl
Division 1
Average height 24–32 in
Flower size Medium to large
Color Pink and white
Flowering time Midsummer
Scent No
Soil type Good, free-draining soil
In the garden Its short stature makes it a good container plant
As a cut flower Charming and attractive

Tiger Babies

This charming and rather classic lily was bred over thirty years ago by award-winning expert Judith Freeman, who set out in the late 1970s to diversify the available garden lilies by introducing new species into the Asiatic lines, through embryo culture. To this end, she took hardy and vigorous Pink Tiger, which had been bred by Leslie Woodriff from parents that are said to include *Lilium regale* and *L. tigrinum*, and crossed it with upright Asiatic lilies. From her accomplished crucible arose the Tiger Babies Group, among very many other notable introductions.

Beautiful, dainty and striking, the heavily spotted flowers fade from a rich apricot center through salmon mousse to dusky pink, with a deeper pink to the back of the petals. The crushed-velvet stamens are held proud of the neat flowers and the impression is one of absolute refinement, which lends itself equally to use in the garden or a vase.

Plant plenty of bulbs so that you can cut the flowers to bring inside or pack them into containers to dot around the terrace.

....

Lilium 'Tiger Babies' (Tiger Babies Group)
Flower type Outward- and downward-facing flowers, with recurved petals and a flat profile
Division 8
Average height 1½–3 ft
Flower size Medium
Color Apricot and blackcurrant
Flowering time Early to midsummer
Scent Delicate
Soil type Fertile and free draining
In the garden The gentle colors of Tiger Babies go with everything, so weave them through borders or enjoy in containers
As a cut flower Classic and elegant

Nymph

Artists can be a dodgy bunch. The French impressionist Pierre-Auguste Renoir is famously quoted as saying "I never think I have finished a nude until I could pinch it." From a jaded, twenty-first-century perspective, this is an unsurprising and typically unreconstructed statement, yet painted nudes have very much informed the popular perception of how a nymph might be. The main perpetrator here, however, is not so much Renoir as Pre-Raphaelite artist John William Waterhouse, and his painting *Hylas and the Nymphs*.

This picture, based on the classical Greek story, depicts young Hylas being tempted to his watery doom by naiads. In their waterlily-filled pool, the nymphs appeal to the tragic youth; they are creatures of beauty, with alabaster skin, dark auburn hair, rosy cheeks and pleading eyes.

The eponymous lily draws on this genre with charm and muted elegance. The fleshy tones of peachy-cream are emphasized by a soft blush at the center of each petal, while the flower emerges from a green puddle of leaves and buds. The flower gazes slightly upwards, both coy and enticing, and possessed of an exotic and alluring cinnamon fragrance.

Nymphs, clearly, are not to be trifled with, and this Orienpet lily grows tall and magnificent once it has settled in. And, although pinching of any sort is ill-advised, it can be cut and arranged with impunity.

....

Lilium 'Nymph'
Flower type An upward-facing bowl with recurved petals
Division 8
Average height 4–6½ ft
Flower size Very large
Color Cream and pink
Flowering time Midsummer
Scent Strongly perfumed, with hints of cinnamon
Soil type Will grow in acid, neutral and alkaline soil, as long as it is well-drained
In the garden A striking back-of-the-border plant; try combining it with the taller pink and purple dahlia varieties
As a cut flower Positively seductive

Star Gazer syn. Stargazer

Certain lilies need no introduction and pretty, fragrant Star Gazer is a household name. As a result of its huge success in the cut-flower trade, we often find ourselves arranging a vase of Stargazers in the same way as we drive a jeep, pour a coke or hoover the carpet.

The original Star Gazer lily was bred in California in the mid-1970s by Leslie Woodriff, a botanical magician and "the father of the Oriental hybrid lily." Here he worked with species lilies with the aim of creating an upward-facing flower rather than a nodding one until a chance genetic mutation produced Star Gazer – and with this he struck gold.

The flamboyant open flower is made up of petals that are hot pink, with a white picotee edge, crimson polka dots and a central stripe that slides into lime-green nectary guides at the heart of the flower. The central stamens are very prominent. The scent is powerful, strong and spicy; some love it, but others can find it completely overwhelming.

Horticulture, however, moves quickly. Plants fade away and new ones replace them. And in the same way that models of the Hoover have evolved since its invention in the 1900s, the name Stargazer is carried forward by a legion of similar plants, both generic and named Orientals, including Special News, Calvados and also Red Eyes (see page 132).

Although often sold as a potted or cut flower, these sturdy Stargazers are good garden plants and perform well in the middle or back of the border, where they generally do not require staking. They look particularly well surrounded by pink, white and blue flowers and silver foliage plants, or paired boldly with orange and bright blue.

....

Lilium 'Star Gazer' syn. 'Stargazer'
Flower type Flattish, upward-facing flowers
Division 7
Average height 3–3½ ft
Flower size Very large
Color Shades of pink and crimson with white edges
Flowering time Mid- to late summer
Scent Heavy and rich
Soil type Humus-rich, acidic and free-draining
In the garden Allow the showstopping flowers to take center stage
As a cut flower One of the best

Lilium pardalinum
syn. Leopard Lily, Panther Lily

While some lily species can be awkward or miffy, *Lilium pardalinum* makes up for its frailties by being refreshingly easy to grow.

The erect stems are frilled with whorls of foliage and topped by a handful of tangerine Turk's caps; the strongly recurved petals are darker orange at the tips but become citrus-gold towards the center, with anthers in a matching hue. The plant is named after the Latin word for leopard, so *pardalinum* refers to the spots on the petals, which are reddish-brown and bordered in orange.

In the wild, it can be found along the Pacific coast of the USA, from Oregon to California and even Mexico and its genes have played an important part in the development of many modern cultivars. Crossing *L. pardalinum* with *L. humboldtii* in the early half of the twentieth century created the now-famous Bellingham Hybrids and their strong subsequent progeny, but the species is a good plant in its own right: tall, robust and with rhizomatous bulbs that form chunky clumps with time.

There are a number of lilies that originate in the damp, western woodlands of America, but *L. pardalinum* is the hardiest and most biddable in the garden. Ideally, it should be planted in moist soil, in sun or part shade; it will grow in drier ground, but the plants will be shorter.

....

Lilium pardalinum
Flower type Downward-facing with recurved petals in the Turk's cap style
Division 9
Average height Variable, it can get to 6½ ft in ideal conditions, but is usually around 3–5 ft
Flower size Medium
Color Flaming orange and yellow, flecked with deep brown
Flowering time High summer
Scent No
Soil type Prefers damp, free-draining soil
In the garden Grow with tall airy grasses such as *Miscanthus* and *Molinia* in sun, hostas and ferns in part shade
As a cut flower Elegant and striking

Viola

Small, beautiful and elegantly frilled, Roselily Viola® is a gorgeous double Oriental bloom. Its petals are shell pink, brushed with a stain of deeper, hotter cerise and with a scatter of dark magenta papillae, while lush ruffles hide the center of the flower entirely. The absence of stamens, and therefore pollen, makes this lily a good choice for allergy sufferers and obviates pollen-staining on surfaces and soft furnishings.

In lily circles, Roselilies are tipped as the next big thing. Earlier varieties such as Roselily Elena® and Roselily Natalia® (see page 48) were pretty and sweet-smelling enough, but newer introductions are reported to be a great improvement. And while the flowers are currently all shades of pink and white, new yellow-, red- and peach-colored varieties are waiting in the wings.

It is possible that Roselily® may follow Stargazer by becoming a generic accepted name for a certain type of flower. The fragrant, ruffled perfection is popular and they are already being imitated. But the name is trademarked, so although the plants of the future may look and smell just like a Roselily®, whether it actually is or not depends on who grows it.

Plant Viola in humus-rich, moist, well-drained soil that tends towards the acidic. As it settles in, it will form neat clumps with the flowers borne on sturdy, feathered stems. Grow alongside a blousy palette of cottage-garden plants or team with bold dahlias, delphiniums or roses, either in the border or in the vase.

A smaller, paler alternative is the unscented Asiatic lily, Elodie.

....

Lilium Roselily Viola®
Flower type Upward- and outward-facing double
Division 7
Average height 3 ft
Flower size Very large
Color Pale pink and cerise
Flowering time Midsummer
Scent Strong, sweet, bubblegum scent
Soil type Ideally slightly acidic
In the garden Perfect for pots and small gardens
As a cut flower Excels with other open lilies, in shades of pink and rose, or use as part of a loose bouquet with *Liatris*, lisianthus, roses and foliage

Trebbiano syn. Gerrit Zalm

With legions of yellow and orange lilies available, the dedicated lily lover might consider themselves well served by both plant and color. But Trebbiano is different.

In its coloring it is subtle, particular, even peculiar. A choleric shade, greenish rather than sunny. It is a hue that hints of unripe lemon rather than true lime, perhaps, but it is unusual and beguiling rather than bilious.

In truth, Trebbiano is named for an Italian white grape used in winemaking, the color evoking the green, yellow, gray-bloomed qualities of the fruit. Rounded petals that are reminiscent of unsalted butter, sliding into virescence at the base, punctuated with the burnt sawdust of the anthers and a pop of puce at the tip of the stigma.

Robust and floriferous, Trebbiano has a lot to recommend it in the garden or cut for the house. Pack into pots for the terrace or cut by the armful to arrange in a summer setting, where its crisp, cool freshness is intensified when offset by white or Delft blue.

....

Lilium 'Trebbiano' syn. 'Gerrit Zalm'
Flower type Open and upward-facing
Division 8
Average height 32–36 in
Flower size Very large
Color Lime green
Flowering time Midsummer
Scent Slight
Soil type Good garden soil, unfussy about pH
In the garden Compact enough for containers and will shine in front of dark foliage or plant with acid green *Euphorbia schillingii* and *Deschampsia flexuosa* for a cool look in part shade
As a cut flower Combine with bright pinks and blues and deep, rich purples for an energetic arrangement

Apricot Fudge

There is a good tradition of naming lilies after delicious and indulgent treats, but this little sweetie will get florists and gardeners salivating in other ways, too.

On paper it is a double *Longiflorum* × Asiatic hybrid: so far, so good. But it is also unusual and exciting, defying convention or perhaps even defining a new genre. Unlike the flamboyant, exotic drama queens that go through life with petals akimbo, the flowers of Apricot Fudge are compact and shell-like, the short, peachy petals curved inwards to create a form that is reminiscent of a tulip or an opening rosebud. Above these the anthers are held upright, like chocolate sprinkles over creamy fruit sorbet.

The plant is compact, so it works well in containers and at the front of the border, while the *Longiflorum* parentage means that it is daintily fragrant. With quiet coloring and modest proportions, these flowers lack the brashness of some of their lily brethren and fit prettily into posies and floral arrangements without stealing the show.

....

Lilium 'Apricot Fudge'
Flower type Upward-facing double
Division 8
Average height 28–32 in
Flower size Small
Color A warm, caramel orange
Flowering time Early to midsummer
Scent Rather delicious
Soil type Any good garden soil
In the garden Fits sweetly in with other summer staples and compact enough to use in containers
As a cut flower Versatile in a vase and small enough to be part of a bridal bouquet

Fiery
and Fabulous

Miss Feya

Orienpets are designed to be fabulous and striking, but even in the face of strong competition from her siblings, Miss Feya is a flower to be reckoned with.

For starters, the color is fabulous: black cherry with notes of port and ice-cream. Then, the tiered chandeliers of flowers are spectacular, glorious and eye-catching. Finally, the scent is exquisite, the perfume of saints and angels.

In the garden, this paragon performs, too, growing taller year upon year until it reaches its substantial mature height, sometimes over 6½ feet. Although a stake may be advised in a windier spot, the stems are strong and, whether scattered through a mixed border or planted in pride of place by the patio, the bodacious blooms of Miss Feya will be a joy to behold.

....

Lilium 'Miss Feya'
Flower type Downward-facing or slightly outward-facing, flat with reflexed petals
Division 8
Average height 4–8 ft
Flower size Very large
Color Rich cherry red with maroon spots
Flowering time Late summer to early autumn
Scent Fragrant
Soil type Unfussy about pH, but likes well-drained soil
In the garden Plant with hot pink or rich blue flowers in the border or position outside a window to enjoy from indoors
As a cut flower Opulent and fabulous

Heartstrings

Heartstrings is a lily that has a kind of vintage quality to it. The apricot and raspberry-sherbet petals, the cutely defined freckles, the studied innocence and prettiness all packed up in a flower that is reminiscent of 1950s America, with Buddy Holly playing on the jukebox in a diner, and girls in swing dresses sipping soda.

Viewed objectively, the bloom is bred to the point where it could almost be a little contrived – like watching the film *Grease* or a 1980s retrospective: the colors are too bright, the styling too on point and the hairstyles too hilarious, in the way that history never is when you are living it. There will be a smutty comment from "the slutty one" and a flying car along any minute now.

But, fortunately, we don't have to live in an ersatz diner or a reconstruction of a Bollywood wedding, and that being so, let us embrace Heartstrings for her charms. After all, she needs no pathos or sympathy, she is quite pretty and bold enough to hold her own and will bring a welcome splash of energy to a white dining room, or tone deliciously with caramel cushions and pink-patterned bedspreads.

Arrange the stems in matching or eclectic vases along a mantelpiece, or mute and max the colors with rich purple, soft gray and every shade of blue. Bring Heartstrings® into harmony with your being and enjoy her for all that she is.

....

Lilium 'Heartstrings'
Flower type Upward-facing flat bowl
Division 1
Average height 3–4 ft
Flower size Large
Color Pink and peach-yellow
Flowering time High summer
Scent Unscented
Soil type Free-draining garden soil
In the garden Plant alongside pink and orange flowers or team with blue and pink delphiniums
As a cut flower Needs no accompaniment

Red Eyes

The Stargazer family of lilies is wide and well known. If not royalty, then it is at the very least accorded film star or cult rocker status by the masses, and as a true scion of the house, Red Eyes does not disappoint.

The neatly frilled picotee petals are a rich, saturated shade of pink, freckled with dark crimson and offset by an acid-green central star. The fragrance, meanwhile, is polished and sublime, as one might expect.

The name is perplexing as it brings to mind weeping, or abject dissolution, and there is nothing in the flower's demeanor to suggest such a thing – it is more a bloom of fabulous, futuristic energy. It is a fascinating star in the lily firmament, flying in formation when arranged in a vase.

While Red Eyes excels as a cut flower and can bring a bold shot of energy to a neutrally decorated room, it also does well in the garden. Plant in acid soil in the border or in pots of ericaceous compost as a feature. Alternatively, mix it with other late-summer planting such as *Agastache* 'Blue Fortune', shrubs like *Caryopteris* and the smaller hydrangeas or softly embraced by purple and pink *Symphyotrichum* (formerly the North American asters).

....

Lilium 'Red Eyes'
Flower type Upward-facing in the Stargazer fashion
Division 7
Average height 3 ft
Flower size Very large
Color Pink and deep pink
Flowering time Mid- to late summer
Scent Beautiful, heavy fragrance
Soil type Acidic garden soil or ericaceous compost
In the garden Lovely in containers
As a cut flower One of the best

Viva la Vida

It is too easy to let the glossy, fragrant fantasy of lilies lead you down a soft-focus path of pastels and prettiness, but should you succumb, then Viva la Vida will smash that reverie with style and energy, for it is a force.

Bold butterscotch in color, the shape of each petal is echoed in a spreading splash of deep, freckled crimson, as if the flower were in the possession of a partying, slightly demonic alter-ego, bursting through to take over not only the bloom but, potentially, the garden.

Yet, as an AOA lily it is an adaptable plant, and not entirely monstrous in origin. An AOA lily is created by crossing an Asiatic hybrid lily with an Oriental, which is then crossed again with an Asiatic, hence the acronym. The resulting flowers are larger than an Asiatic, with elegantly reflexed petals and a subtle scent that is softer than an Oriental, while the color combinations are unique.

In the garden, team this sultry beauty with plants that will emphasize its striking good looks. Plummy foliage shrubs such as *Physocarpus opulifolius* 'Diabolo' and *Pittosporum tenuifolium* 'Tom Thumb' will highlight the damson undertones at its heart. Meanwhile, its jammy apricot-marmalade qualities can be emphasized by pairing it with other orange flowers such as *Kniphofia* and *Crocosmia*, and a cooler look can be attained by combining with deep greens, purples and cobalt blues.

Smaller, darker alternatives include Asiatic lilies Forever Susan and Easy Samba.

....

Lilium 'Viva la Vida'
Flower type Upward- and outward-facing bowl
Division 8
Average height 3–4 ft
Flower size Very large
Color Butterscotch yellow and burnt raspberry
Flowering time Early to midsummer
Scent Slight perfume
Soil type Unfussy, likes good, well-drained garden soil
In the garden An eye-catching plant for the middle of the border and compact enough to grow in pots on the patio
As a cut flower Bold and striking

Mascara

A lauded "black" Asiatic hybrid, Mascara combines its commitment to the goth-horror genre of flower gardening with a well-defined sense of fun.

Quite the little vamp, it produces evocative *Little Shop of Horrors* buds that expand into a thing of dark beauty. The tones are inky with blood and iniquity, but the hint of ginger implies an irony that is far more *Rocky Horror Picture Show* than *Dracula*.

In addition to dramatic good looks, Mascara has a robust habit and strong stem, adding pizzazz, impact and fun in the garden. It combines beautifully with potentillas and orange geums, as well as pink and purple penstemons and *Knautia macedonica*. Alternatively, underplant with *Eschscholzia californica* or *Alchemilla mollis* for theatrical effect.

···

Lilium 'Mascara'
Flower type Upward- and outward-facing bowl
Division 1
Average height 3 ft
Flower size Large
Color Rich, inky red-purple
Flowering time Midsummer
Scent No
Soil type Any good garden soil
In the garden Will pop when planted with hot oranges and strong pinks, or can be used to anchor a purple and lavender scheme
As a cut flower Rather stunning

Amarossi

A large stand of Amarossi is truly a magnificent sight to behold. A tree lily, or Orienpet, it is the height of a tall man; the chunky stems terminate in a raceme of green buds that pop open one by one, freeing a spray of dark chocolate anthers that stand proud of the wide, bold bloom.

The flowers are a meditation on the splendor of the color pink. It is deep fuchsia, hot coral, wine-red, cherry, sepia-paprika, raspberry lemonade. It is clear ruby and mulberry vodka. It is all of these in tones, depths and highlights, that gently evolve as the flower opens and ages.

At the base of each petal there is a flash of green and a smudge of cream, with a few freckles to remind us that the flower is real rather than made of silk, yet it has a glowing, almost iridescent quality, and a sheen to the petals that calls even this into question.

But if you like a pink lily that is packed with character and pizzazz, then Amarossi is the one for you. And while they can be cut in armfuls for an indoor arrangement, plant them against a pale blue wall and the color will absolutely pop.

Lilium 'Amarossi'
Flower type An outward-facing, flattish sort of flower
Division 8
Average height 32–60 in
Flower size Very large
Color Fuchsia and coral
Flowering time Midsummer onwards
Scent Deliciously fragrant
Soil type Unfussy, but likes well-drained soil
In the garden Stands bold at the back of the border, and is even bolder used as a statement plant against a building or boundary; plant with *Miscanthus sinensis* var. *condensatus* 'Cosmopolitan' and *Persicaria alpina* for complement and contrast
As a cut flower Lavish and opulent

Arabian Knight

A name like Arabian Knight engenders a certain amount of expectation. It resonates with classic tales of handsome fellows on proudly muscled steeds, the rider exotically clad in flowing robes and rich brocades, turban on their head and scimitar in hand; the horse a vision of power and restraint.

It comes with the cultural echoes of Turkey and the Middle East, as a pinnacle of sophistication, culture and learning – and not inconsiderable romance.

And the flower itself does not disappoint. It has the coloring – a rich mahogany-maroon, overlaying a seam of old gold and elegantly coordinated anthers. It also has the evocative Turk's cap shape and performs robustly in the garden, just as a Martagon hybrid should.

Of course, and almost inevitably, the lily Arabian Knight is also known as Arabian Night – which is literally, a classic tale, a narrative of lust, murder and a woman facing adversity and prevailing through her stories and intelligence. But no matter, this is a lily that will sweep you off your feet.

....

Lilium 'Arabian Knight'
Flower type Turk's cap
Division 2
Average height Variable, 4¼–5 ft
Flower size Small
Color Rich, inky purple with burnt-orange highlights
Flowering time Early to midsummer
Scent Fragrant
Soil type Good, well-drained soil; will tolerate chalk
In the garden Pick up the smoldering tones with other purple and orange flowers, such as *Salvia* 'Amistad' or 'Caradonna', and *Geum* 'Flames of Passion' and 'Totally Tangerine'
As a cut flower Bold and good-looking

Lady Alice

If you were to create a flower that was inspired by a ginger tabby kitten – rather than the more traditional tiger or leopard that is normally associated with lilies – you might end up with Lady Alice.

A hybrid of *Lilium henryi*, the papillae in Lady Alice are very pronounced, forming a kind of fleshy orange fur, and the petals are strongly reflexed. The coloring is more or less tangerine and vanilla with ochre speckles, and each demure bud opens in turn, to reveal a cluster of bronze-rust anthers hanging beneath the flower.

The flower is cheerful and fresh in demeanor and, just like the tiger lily that Alice meets in Wonderland, it is perfectly reasonable in attitude – growing well with the other garden plants (even if they are foolish and rude, such as some of those encountered by the other Alice) It looks particularly good when combined with other tall, orange or purple Turk's cap lilies, or threaded through a tropical-themed planting scheme.

....

Lilium 'Lady Alice'
Flower type Outward- and downward-facing, flattish with reflexed petals
Division 6
Average height 4–5 ft
Flower size Large
Color Orange and white
Flowering time Midsummer
Scent Wonderfully fragrant
Soil type Prefers good soil, but otherwise unfussy
In the garden Beautiful threaded through the border with *Iris sibirica* and grasses or nodding over a fence
As a cut flower Simple and elegant

Chocolate Event

A very unusual-looking lily, Chocolate Event is part of the Event Series of lilies, including Strawberry Event and Stracciatella Event, and it is really rather scrumptious.

The color is intriguing, blending together burgundy, copper and peach in a way that creates that slightly split effect you get when making ganache, just as the double cream is poured into rich, dark, molten chocolate and stirred.

As an Asiatic it may not be scented, yet it is redolent of luxury. It has the look of intense and fruity cocoa, with the reddish-black character that indicates really good quality; it has creamy, high-calorie stamens and anthers that are speckled with gold leaf.

In the garden Chocolate Event increases well in sun or part shade, and looks lovely combined with dark red, orange or purple flowers that will pick up its core colors, or its charms can be emphasized with a clean foil of green foliage. Equally, it can be brought inside and given pride of place in a vase.

Lilium 'Chocolate Event'
Flower type Open, outward-facing to slightly pendent
Division 1
Average height 4 ft
Flower size Large
Color Copper, burgundy and cream
Flowering time Early to midsummer
Scent None
Soil type Good neutral or alkaline garden soil
In the garden Perfect in a large container at the edge of a patio or deck where the unique coloring can be appreciated
As a cut flower Striking in a vase

Pink Flight

While pink flowers often run the risk of being brash, sugary or insipid, Pink Flight is the very epitome of sophisticated. The deep, slightly dusty rose color is confident, yet at the same time it manages not to be overbearing, while the wash of lemon-cream that is brushed into its throat softens the flower and offsets its slender fuchsia stamens rather nicely.

Held up on sturdy stems, the flowers are large and poised and the slightly recurved petals create a swooping effect, as if in reality the flower might be some exotic bird, circling in to land on an invisible lake.

In the garden, this floriferous Asiatic lily rises fairly early by the standards of its kind and puts on a good show, either by itself in a nice pot, or combined with other flowers and foliage in the border.

....

Lilium 'Pink Flight'
Flower type Flattish, outward-facing flowers with slightly recurved petals
Division 1
Average height 3–4 ft
Flower size Large
Color A sumptuous blend of coral and raspberry
Flowering time Early to midsummer
Scent Unscented
Soil type Free-draining alkaline soil or multipurpose compost
In the garden Weave through the herbaceous border, where it will combine well with perennials such as phlox, penstemons and echinaceas; alternatively, grow in containers
As a cut flower A sophisticated addition to an arrangement

Lilium henryi

This species lily was named after Professor Augustine Henry, an Irish plant hunter who was traveling along the Yangtze River near Yichang, in 1888, when he spotted it growing on the limestone cliffs of the Wu Gorge.

An extremely popular garden plant, its long stems are topped with between four and twenty dancing orange flowers. The strongly reflexed petals are covered with fleshy papillae, and at the center of the bloom, the long and prominent stamens are tipped with small, rusty anthers. The color of the flowers is variable – sometimes more apricot and sometimes more caramel – but whatever the hue, maroon freckles add depth and bass notes, and this prevents the orange from being too light and carroty.

Originating in a calcareous landscape, *Lilium henryi* is tolerant of lime soils, although it will also thrive in neutral ground. It is stem-rooting, so it needs to be planted at least 8 inches deep. Keep an eye on it in late winter and spring as it can start into growth early in the season, and young shoots will need to be protected if there is a late frost.

Choose a location in part shade, where the roots will be cool and the soil does not dry out. While growth may be weak for the first couple of years, once the flower gets into its stride, the stems can reach over 5 feet tall, so staking may be necessary. Alternatively, plant it among shrubs that will afford it a certain amount of support.

Lilium henryi was given an Award of Garden Merit by the Royal Horticultural Society in 1993.

....

Lilium henryi
Flower type Turk's cap
Division 9
Average height 4–8 ft
Flower size Medium
Color Warm orange, speckled with maroon
Flowering time Late summer
Scent Unscented
Soil type Free-draining, alkaline to neutral
In the garden Excels in light woodland or in the border alongside blue *Echinops* or rich pink echinaceas, but it does not perform well in pots
As a cut flower A spare and striking accent plant

Red Velvet

With sumptuous petals of the richest, deepest, carmine red, discreetly stippled with black-purple papillae and anthers of gold-brushed amber, this deservedly popular lily brings to mind nights at the theatre, moistly delicious cake and passionate liaisons in flower form.

Red Velvet is an Asiatic hybrid that was created by the famous lily-breeding duo David Stone and F. Henry Payne. Stone became a recognized expert and lectured on hybridizing throughout America, and together with horticulturist and fellow hybridizer Payne, he pursued his ambition of producing Asiatic lilies without spots, developing the well-known series of Connecticut hybrids en route.

To this end, they worked with every spotless lily that they could lay their hands on, and back-crossed with several true species, building into their work a vigor and disease-resistance that has been of benefit to lily growers ever since. Eminent hybridizer Jan de Graaff purchased many of their excellent hybrids in the 1960s.

Leave Red Velvet to naturalize in the garden and it should come back bigger and better each year. Team with grasses and perennials in the border or cluster with hardy palms, dahlias, cannas and *Ricinus* for a colorful and exotic display.

....

Lilium 'Red Velvet'
Flower type Slightly pendent star
Division 1
Average height 3–4¼ ft
Flower size Medium
Color Deep, blood-red
Flowering time Late summer
Scent Unscented
Soil type Any good garden soil
In the garden Use to add depth and drama to a tropical scheme or soften with orange flowers and airy grasses
As a cut flower Bold and very lovely

Lilium superbum

With all the sophistication and impact of a garden cultivar, and all the elegance and lightness-of-being of a wildflower, *Lilium superbum* is native to the eastern USA, favoring wet meadows and woodlands in a wide swathe that follows the Appalachian Mountains, from New Hampshire to Florida.

The epithet *superbum* is the Latin for "proud" or "excellent," and while the individual flowers are small, they are striking. Carried in airy clusters at the end of long stems, the bright blooms are boldly marked with spots and flames and sport a central green star. The petals are strongly reflexed and cinnamon-colored anthers hover below the bloom.

The plant spreads and multiplies via underground stolons, and in the wild it may form magnificent clumps, although it is endangered or vulnerable in a number of areas. In gardens, it is not always easy to establish and can fall prey to virus, but it can do well once it gets going.

Due to its extensive distribution, this lily shows considerable natural variation. It can produce between twelve and forty blooms, and its color ranges from orange-yellow to deep orange-red. It can also vary significantly in height.

Historically, the bulbs of *Lilium superbum* were used as a source of food by Native Americans, and the flowers attract nectar-lovers and pollinators, including hummingbirds, where they are present. Vernacular names include Turk's cap lily, great American Turk's cap lily, turban lily and swamp lily and it can sometimes be referred to as a tiger lily, although it is a different species to the Asian plant of the same name.

....

Lilium superbum
Flower type Turk's cap
Division 9
Average height Variable, 4–8 ft
Flower size Small
Color Deep-gold to orange-red flowers are heavily spotted with maroon
Flowering time High summer
Scent Unscented
Soil type Moist by the standards of most lilies, humus-rich and lime-free
In the garden Use informally in full or part sun
As a cut flower Very attractive

Majestic
and Magnificent

African Queen

First introduced in 1958, African Queen – or African Queen Group, as the closely related clones are properly known – is a titan among lilies. The flower stems of a well-established clump can reach over 5 feet tall, each one boasting up to twenty blooms, which open sequentially for a long-lasting display.

The magnificent, slightly pendent trumpet flowers are rich and enticing in hue – the petals are burnt orange with hints of caramel, and washed with raspberry-bronze to the reverse. The prominent stigma is ringed with butterscotch anthers and the flowers are sweetly and deliciously scented.

This is a plant that is not to be faulted in its poise and impact; it can be planted in state at the back of the border in a sheltered position – use a stake if in doubt. Sink the bulbs at least 6 inches deep in moist, free-draining soil; pots are an option but they do need to be substantial to accommodate the roots and for the full-grown plant to be stable. This lily does not mind a little shade and is unfussy about soil pH, within reason.

African Queen received an eminently well-deserved Award of Garden Merit from the Royal Horticultural Society in 2002.

. . . .

Lilium 'African Queen' (African Queen Group)
Flower type Outward or downward-facing trumpet
Division 6
Average height 4–5 ft
Flower size Large
Color Deep apricot with a garnet reverse
Flowering time High summer
Scent Beautiful and intoxicating
Soil type Humus-rich and free-draining
In the garden A handsome back-of-the-border plant
As a cut flower Striking and statuesque, if you have a large enough vase

Casa Blanca

Standing tall, proud and elegant, Casa Blanca is a vision of perfection and it doesn't care who knows it.

The elongated buds that nestle among the glossy foliage are the sort of faint pink, green and cream that is normally associated with magnolias, but when they burst they slough off such subtleties. The flowers are magnificent: sweetly fragrant and peerlessly white, save for a hint of green in the depths.

Each bloom is held wide and open, the petals delicately reflexed at the tips, while a scatter of puckered, spiky papillae at the base provides an edgy, textured quality and a sense of style. Meanwhile, at the end of light green stamens, cinnamon and sumac-colored anthers are thrust brazenly outward in such a fashion that a passing pollinator could be forgiven for doing a double-take before diving in.

One of the oldest Oriental hybrids, Casa Blanca was introduced in 1984 and holds an Award of Garden Merit from the Royal Horticultural Society. Fully hardy, it will do well in a sunny spot with well-drained soil, ideally enriched with a little leaf mold.

Lilium 'Casa Blanca'
Flower type Outward-facing, flattish bowl
Division 7
Average height 4 ft
Flower size Large
Color Purest white with bold, brick-red stamens
Flowering time High summer to late summer
Scent Gloriously fragrant
Soil type Humus-rich and lime-free
In the garden A bold statement flower that is particularly striking against a painted wall or fence
As a cut flower Beautiful combined with foliage such as ferny asparagus or gray-blue eucalyptus

Silk Road

Towering and glorious, Silk Road is nothing if not flamboyant. Its pillar of flowers brings to mind a fantasy of the Orient: tales of trade and daring exploits between European countries and the exotic East, and in the other direction, too. It recalls Chinese textiles, images of peonies, chrysanthemums and cherry blossom, epitomizing all that is desirable, expensive and tantalizing.

This Orienpet has strong stems, each stacked with torpedo-shaped buds that burst one after the other to reveal glossy, fragrant flowers that, while ostensibly white, are marked with a dramatic, dark pink splotch, like a glass of cabernet sauvignon knocked onto a snowy tablecloth.

In the garden it establishes quickly and, with a moderate tendency to eclipse surrounding plants, in many ways it needs no accompaniment. It looks lovely planted at the back of a mixed border, perhaps against a wall that is painted in a contrasting color. Alternatively, array these handsome blooms along a boundary where they can nod over the railings and provide a talking point for passers-by.

Lilium 'Silk Road'
Flower type Wide-open trumpet
Division 8
Average height 5–8 ft
Flower size Very large
Color White and crimson-pink
Flowering time Mid- to late summer
Scent Prettily perfumed
Soil type Unfussy, but well-drained preferred
In the garden An eye-catching border specimen which works well with tall grasses
As a cut flower Spectacular

Yelloween

While spring brings a scatter of sunny daffodils and primroses, with summer comes lilies and Yelloween is one of the most cheerful and gently charming blonde bombshells in a crowded field.

Produced by Dutch breeder Pieter Jan Kos, who crossed an Aurelian hybrid – a group of lilies that have the genes of both Chinese Trumpet lilies and *L. henryi* – with an Oriental lily, Yelloween is a tall plant and the flowers are correspondingly large. The green buds break to reveal flowers that are a tangy, buttery, lemon-curd hue but are refined by lime highlights, a rich lime center and contrasting, and rather elegant, bitter-chocolate anthers.

Plant in the middle or back of a border where its roots can be in cool, well-drained, slightly acidic soil, while the sweetly scented flowers bask in the sun and enjoy the attentions of bees and butterflies. A mulch over winter and just a little food in early spring will do it a power of good and it will get taller as it becomes more established.

Cut the flowers as the first buds start to open and they will last up to ten days in a vase, where they combine beautifully with foliage and roses.

....

Lilium 'Yelloween'
Flower type Upward-facing, open trumpet
Division 8
Average height 3–8 ft
Flower size Very large
Color Pale yellow
Flowering time High summer
Scent Fragrant
Soil type Moisture-rich, well-drained and acidic
In the garden Plant as an extended group along a wall or hedge, or as clumps among taller and later-flowering herbaceous perennials in the border
As a cut flower A complete showstopper

Lilium regale

While some lilies could be considered awkward or even vexatious in the garden, delightful *Lilium regale* is a species that is not only magnificent to look at, but also satisfyingly easy to grow. Encountered in 1903 by legendary plant hunter Ernest "Chinese" Wilson in the Min Valley, Sichuan Province, China, he wrote of this flower:

"There, in narrow, semi-arid valleys, down which thunder torrents, and encompassed by mountains composed of mud-shales and granites, whose peaks are clothed with snow eternal, the Regal Lily has its home. In summer the heat is terrific, in winter the cold is intense, and at all seasons these valleys are subject to sudden and violent wind-storms … There, in June, by the wayside, in rock-crevices by the torrent's edge, and high up on the mountainside and precipice, this lily in full bloom greets the weary wayfarer. Not in twos and threes but in hundreds, in thousands, aye, in tens of thousands."

Returning to the valley to collect further specimens Wilson was caught in a mudslide and broke his leg. The story goes that the train of forty mules had to be led clear, each one stepping over him, before his porters could splint the injury with the legs of his camera tripod. However, the leg set badly and Wilson carried his "lily limp" for the rest of his life.

Despite this wild birth, blackcurrant-stained *L. regale* and its white form, *L. regale* 'Album' (see pages 180–81) are supremely popular garden plants. Variable in height, the species produces deep-purple buds, opening into white trumpets around 5½ inches long.

Plant the stem-rooting bulbs at around 8 inches deep in good soil and don't overfeed.

....

Lilium regale
Flower type Trumpet
Division 9
Average height Variable, up to 5 ft
Flower size Large
Color White flowers with a yellow throat
Flowering time Midsummer
Scent Sweet, floral and delicious
Soil type Well-drained and humus-rich, will tolerate chalk
In the garden Combine in the border with other tall spires such as delphiniums, the larger salvias or shrubs, *Ammi majus*, foxgloves, *Verbena bonariensis* and alliums
As a cut flower Glamorous, if heavily scented

Purple Prince

This striking and handsome flower is what we have come to expect from lilies in recent years. It is an Orienpet – an Oriental-Trumpet, or OT, hybrid – and it is one of the group known as tree lilies, which, when established, are reputed to reach 6½–8 feet tall. And although the realistic among us might moderate our expectations according to growing conditions, it is a majestic plant that's likely to achieve head height at least.

Resembling green-streaked, purple torpedoes, the buds expand and break to reveal huge, glorious, waxy flowers. The gorgeous, rich purple color is offset by lime-green nectary furrows in the center and hot-orange anthers, while the long, recurved petals form an open, flared trumpet. Thanks to their heritage, these particular lily flowers are sweetly but not overpoweringly fragrant.

Purple Prince may take a bit of time to settle in and reach its full garden potential, but it should get bigger and better year on year. Plant it in a sunny or partly shaded spot, treat it well and leave it undisturbed, and when it does achieve its peak performance it will be a sight to behold.

....

Lilium 'Purple Prince'
Flower type Trumpet
Division 8
Average height Tall: 6½–8 ft
Flower size Very large
Color Rich royal purple
Flowering time Midsummer
Scent Sweetly fruity
Soil type Any good garden soil
In the garden Use as a statement flower to add drama and height to an herbaceous border, although it is too large for most containers
As a cut flower Versatile and striking, it is the sort of purple color that goes with almost anything

Zelmira

There is something achingly sumptuous about the flowers of Zelmira. It could be the almost shell-like translucence that causes the flower to glow when the sun is low in the sky; it could be the gentle subtleties of a bloom the color of watered peach silk that is offset by arsenic-green nectaries and burnt-brown anthers.

It is, in short, the sort of flower that begs you to don silk pajamas and collapse on a crisp four-poster bed, a spray of flowers in one hand and a romantic novel in the other, and wait for your lover to come.

Rather appropriately, therefore, the name Zelmira comes from a rather complicated opera by Rossini. The titular heroine is the daughter of Polidoro, the beloved but aging King of Lesbos. With her husband engaged in battle elsewhere, a former suitor, Azor, invades the island to take over the throne. But in a series of clever twists, Zelmira hides her father and the usurping Azor is killed by a second aspirant king, Antenore, who then frames her for trying to kill her husband, Ilo, and she is imprisoned.

Fortune follows misfortune and opportunity follows treachery and eventually Zelmira and her father are rescued and her marriage is saved. The bad guys are led off in chains and the good guys live happily ever after. Which, in romance, life and lilies is pretty much all anyone could want.

Lilium 'Zelmira'
Flower type Upward- and outward-facing bowl
Division 8
Average height 3–6½ ft
Flower size Very large
Color Glowing peach
Flowering time Mid- to late summer
Scent Very rich perfume
Soil type Any good, well-drained garden soil
In the garden Looks well teamed with gentle purples, such as *Dahlia* 'Thomas A. Edison', or experiment with splashes of fresh green
As a cut flower Excellent and highly sophisticated

Triumphator syn. Zanlophator

Some plants naturally exude a sense of cheerfulness, and lily Triumphator, with its large, gaily colored trumpets and upright form, might just be the sunniest and most good-natured of them all.

While the flowers are pretty individually, when massed together Triumphator gives the impression of an avalanche of raspberry-ripple ice cream. Each bold and handsome trumpet bursts from its long, slightly alien bud to reveal a white flower, heavily stained with rich, red wine. At the center of the flower, prominent cream stamens bear plush ginger anthers, which surround an upward-facing tricorn stigma.

One of the newer Orienpet varieties, this lily is vigorous and hardy and does best when planted in averagely good soil that is moist but not waterlogged, although it will also perform in a large container. In shade or on a more exposed site, staking may be advised.

....

Lilium 'Triumphator' syn. 'Zanlophator'
Flower type Upward-facing, open trumpet
Division 8
Average height 3–5 ft
Flower size Large to very large
Color White with a bold pink center
Flowering time Mid- to late summer
Scent Outrageously good
Soil type Good and free-draining
In the garden A cheerful and high-impact subject for a midsummer border; flowers may be slightly smaller if grown in pots
As a cut flower Splendiferous

Beijing Moon

Epitomizing everything that we love about the genus *Lilium*, Beijing Moon is both impressive and gorgeous.

The vast, glorious, pagoda-shaped trumpets are soft in hue, a nuanced rose-lavender pink that gently gives way to glowing yellow at the center of the flower. The thick petals have a subtle sheen that brings to mind exquisite vintage silks from China.

Beloved by bees and flower arrangers alike, Beijing Moon is unfussy about soil as long as the drainage is on point, and it thrives in sunshine, although it will take a little shade. It is an Aurelian hybrid, which has become a blanket term for all hybrids of Chinese Trumpet lily species and *L. henryi*.

Plant in a place where the bulbs can remain undisturbed and the display will get bigger and better, year after year. A mulch of well-rotted organic material can be beneficial in cooler areas.

....

Lilium 'Beijing Moon'
Flower type Slightly flat trumpet, facing outwards and downwards
Division 6
Average height 4–6½ ft
Flower size Very large
Color Pink and pale pink with yellow
Flowering time Mid- and late summer
Scent The strong fragrance is reminiscent of jasmine
Soil type Good soil, unfussy about pH
In the garden A magnificent focal point among herbaceous perennials
As a cut flower Exquisite

Candy Club

The longer a healthy clump of lilies is left to grow, the larger the plants tend to get. And when the Orienpet lily Candy Club is first planted, one might be forgiven for thinking that describing this big-bloomed upstart as a tree lily might be over-egging things somewhat.

Left to its own devices, however, like the giant turnip of fairy-tale fame, it will grow and grow and grow, which brings us on to the secondary incongruity: its sweet and childish name. Candy Club sounds like something on Saturday morning kids' TV, all bright colors and bouncy presenters with a tendency to burst into song. A long way, in fact, from the towering pink-and-white triffid that the eponymous lily becomes.

In late summer, Candy Club erupts into magnificent bloom, a skyscraper of gigantic flowers in a palette of very un-monstrous cream and white. It likes a soil that is nutritious and free-draining, but it will take a bit of clay if it must, and don't forget to stake it in its third year, if not before.

Tree lilies are popular and Candy Club is a bit of a sweetie both in the border and, if you too are big and brave, it is fabulous cut in a bouquet.

Lilium 'Candy Club'
Flower type Outward-facing bowl
Division 8
Average height 3–6 ft
Flower size Very large
Color Cream, pink and still darker pink
Flowering time Mid- to late summer
Scent Classic lily fragrance
Soil type Decent, well-drained soil
In the garden Holds court on its own, or combine with other tall planting at the back of the border
As a cut flower A big flower for big rooms and big vases

Eastern Moon

While some lilies are brash and brilliant party pieces – all hot colors, high contrasts and waving their double-ruffled petticoats at the sky – sweet, blushing Eastern Moon speaks of modesty and refinement.

Expanding from puce buds, the flowers dip demurely to form nodding trumpets of remarkable slenderness and elegance. The external midrib remains a rich gray-raspberry while the inner petals fade to a lighter and whiter pink-magnolia. The heart of the flower is immaculate; the fragrant, gold-painted depths smooth and perfect, unmarred by freckles, speckles, spots or fleshy excrescences.

It is romantic, too, and it could, with a modicum of imagination, be likened to a cluster of gentle moons, rising in the lavender light of a midsummer sky; the sunset ebbing slowly and the heavens transforming from pink to purple as the stars hold back the eventual darkness.

The stems are strong and the plant performs well in the garden, and also cuts impeccably for an indoor arrangement.

Eastern Moon is also known as Easter Moon and Eastern Morn.

....

Lilium 'Eastern Moon'
Flower type Outward- and downward-facing open trumpet
Division 6
Average height 4–6 ft
Flower size Very large
Color Dusty rose and yellow
Flowering time Mid- to late summer
Scent Scented
Soil type Good, well-drained soil
In the garden Use informally as a woodland-edge or back-of-the-border plant, or display in large tubs
As a cut flower Sublime and sophisticated

Zambesi

Poised, pure and exquisite in every way, easy-going Orienpet Zambesi is packed with charm and personality.

Save for a hint of green around the nectaries, Zambesi is a clear, uncomplicated white: it is the lily that goes with anything. In a heavy-bottomed vase, it makes a bold and clean statement, ideal to freshen up and perfume a room. In the garden, meanwhile, the huge flowers sit in the summer border like fat, glossy snowflakes that have been crafted from royal icing and that have unaccountably landed among the greenery.

In either situation, it looks fantastic against the inky foliage of plants such as *Cotinus coggygria* 'Royal Purple' or with acid-green hostas; team it with wine-red roses and salvias and counterpoint the oversized blooms with smaller white flowers, such as those of geraniums, *Gaura* and *Gypsophila*. It will even take the orange of plants such as *Crocosmia* × *crocosmiiflora* 'Emily McKenzie', as long as the surrounding colors are reasonably restrained.

....

Lilium 'Zambesi'®
Flower type Forward-facing open trumpet
Division 8
Average height 4–6 ft
Flower size Very large
Color White
Flowering time Midsummer
Scent Smells a little like marshmallow
Soil type Good, well-drained garden soil; unfussy about pH
In the garden Very dramatic; use in large tubs near seating areas and in formal or minimalist gardens
As a cut flower Makes a powerful statement

African Lady

Derived from the cross-breeding of an Oriental with *Lilium nepalense*, African Lady is an impressive creature indeed.

L. nepalense is a real showpiece – a stoloniferous bulb that produces incredibly dramatic flowers. The long, pendent trumpets flare abruptly outwards to create an implausibly wide mouth to the bloom. Each long petal curls tightly back upon itself and the yellow color of the tips switches abruptly to a dark mahogany as it vanishes into the tube of the trumpet.

So, through the miracle of genetic recombination African Lady is a very showy and impressive flower. Robust, easy to grow and not too tall, the huge flowers are elegantly poised, with petals that are thick and almost rubbery in texture.

The dark central mark of *L. nepalense* has become diluted and extended in its offspring, now covering most of the flower in coppery maroon, with just a residue of yellow at the petal margins and the tips.

Plant in blocks in the garden for maximum drama or weave generously through hot-colored planting schemes.

....

Lilium 'African Lady'
Flower type Flattish, outward-facing flowers
Division 8
Average height 32–50 in
Flower size Very large
Color Orange and copper-red
Flowering time Mid- to late summer
Scent Strong, rich perfume
Soil type Good garden soil
In the garden Fabulous in a hot border with crocosmias, monardas and *Lobelia cardinalis* 'Queen Victoria'
As a cut flower Very bold and striking

LILY
GROWING AND CARE

LILIES ARE BEAUTIFUL, INTOXICATING AND EVOCATIVE, YET IN
INNOCENT HANDS THEY CAN PRESENT A CHALLENGE. SOME ARE PARTICULAR
ABOUT LIME, WHILE OTHERS ARE DEMANDING ABOUT THE DEPTH AT WHICH
THEY ARE PLANTED. AND THEN THERE IS THE MENACE OF LILY BEETLE
TO CONTEND WITH, A FIEND IN SCARLET LIVERY. BUT GET IT RIGHT
AND LILIES CAN GROW HAPPILY AND VIGOROUSLY, MULTIPLYING
WELL AND EXCELLING IN CONTAINERS, CAPTIVATING ONLOOKERS
WITH THEIR BRILLIANCE AND CHARM.

Cultivation

In general, lilies do well when planted in full sun or dappled shade, although they prefer a cool root-run if possible – heads in the sun, feet in the shade, like clematis, is the rule of thumb. This makes them ideal for growing through shrubs, not only to shade the lower part of the plant but to provide a modicum of support as well.

Soil should be rich, moist and free-draining, and most lilies prefer a pH that is neutral or slightly acid, although some are tolerant of lime. The plants are often tall, so they should be sited somewhere sheltered, and certainly out of the prevailing wind; even so, it can be a good idea to provide stakes or other support, to help keep the leggy stems upright in the breeze.

Climates and soils vary and the species and cultivars can have individual needs, so to get the best display of lilies, and to have them coming back year after year, it is a good idea to get to know your garden, to choose varieties that favor your existing conditions and to prepare the ground as well as possible, to welcome your bulbs in.

Selecting varieties

With some plant genera, it would be logical to list the different species and discuss their preferences and foibles individually, but as a group, lilies are so sprawling and interconnected that in this book it makes more sense to look at common garden situations and indicate which varieties will tolerate or even enjoy each one.

The bulbs tend to prefer a fair bit of sun and cool, moist, free-draining soil and are least tolerant of very dry, very wet and chalky conditions. Yet there are degrees in this as we will see below.

Dappled shade No lilies like deep shade, but many are tolerant of a little, while Martagon lilies will be perfectly happy in the light shade cast by trees and tall shrubs, and they lend themselves to naturalizing in woodland-edge situations. If you are unsure, it is always worth experimenting as long as you avoid close proximity to large, lowering conifers or other heavy evergreens.

Full sun If you can offer your lilies full sun, then do so – they enjoy basking in the bright light, where pollinating insects can easily find them. But the warmer the site, the more careful you should be about creating a cool, moisture-retentive root-run.

Dry ground Lilies hate to dry out completely, (although they prefer some drought to waterlogging), so if your soil is light and dry, apply lashings of mulch to improve the structure and help to retain moisture. The Madonna lily, *Lilium candidum*, particularly favors a drier site.

HARDINESS

There are a range of tables that indicate what level of chill a plant will tolerate. Two useful systems are produced by the United States Department of Agriculture (USDA) and the Royal Horticultural Society (RHS), which range from tropical to extremely cold.

USDA
Zone 3 -40°F to -30°F (-40°C to -34°C)
Zone 4 -30°F to -20°F (-34°C to -29°C)
Zone 5 -20°F to -10°F (-29°C to -23°C)
Zone 6 -10°F to 0°F (-23°C to -18°C)
Zone 7 0°F to 10°F (-18°C to -12°C)
Zone 8 10°F to 20°F (-12°C to -7°C)
Zone 9: 20°F to 30°F (-7°C to -1°C)

RHS
H3 to 23°F (-5°C), half hardy
H4 to 14°F (-10°C), hardy in an average winter
H5 to 5°F (-15°C), hardy in a cold winter
H6 to -4°F (-20°C), hardy in a very cold winter
H7 colder than -4°F (-20°C), very hardy

Many lilies are fully hardy, tolerating chill to approximately USDA 4–8, or RHS H6. Where varieties may be less hardy, this is indicated in the plant profiles on pages 36–201.

Wet or heavy ground

Like many bulbs, lilies
don't like to have
wet feet, and excess
moisture, particularly
when dormant, can cause
the plant to rot, so sharp
drainage is key. Improve
drainage as much as you can
with grit and organic matter;
building a raised mound to help lift
the plants away from the mire can also help.
Leopard lilies and *L. superbum* are tolerant of
wetter soils and may grow taller In moist ground,
but if there is any chance that the lilies will find
themselves sitting in a stagnant puddle in winter,
cut your losses and grow them in pots.

Alkaline soil Many lilies, particularly Orientals,
are deeply unhappy in chalky, limy soil, but
others take it in their stride. Some of the most
tolerant are the Martagon lilies, together with
Lilium henryi, *L. candidum* and *L. regale*,
while the Asiatics, *L. pyrenaicum* and many
Trumpet hybrids, will also put up with a degree
of alkalinity. If you garden on chalk and want to
grow the others, it is best to do so in containers.

Acid soil The majority of lilies, other than Asiatic
hybrids, will be perfectly happy growing in at
least moderately acid soil, but there are some
that absolutely demand a low pH. These include
the Orientals, *Lilium auratum* and cultivars of
L. speciosum.

Buying lilies

Lilies are sold from autumn through to spring and can also be purchased already planted up in containers in mid- to late spring, at which point they will be in growth and preparing to flower.

When bulbs are harvested in the field towards the end of the growing season, the leaves are often still green and the moist, juicy bulbs are highly susceptible to bruising and abrasion. They then need to be stored in a cool, dry, airy place but, because they are not protected by a dry outer skin like some other bulbs, such as daffodils and onions, damage at this stage can lead to decay and they are also at risk of drying out.

The best way to buy your lily bulbs is from a reputable specialist nursery, many of whom will offer a mail-order service. Do this, and you should be confident of receiving large, high-quality bulbs that arrive in good condition, very often with planting instructions from the in-house experts to help ensure success.

Bulbs are often widely available in garden centers and DIY chains, and while these can be attractively priced, you should inspect them carefully for signs of damage or desiccation. If they are shriveled, bruised, moldy or otherwise deteriorating, they are best avoided. Crammed into bins and rifled through by shoppers, they can get bashed around and dry out very easily.

When the bulbs are brought out of cold store onto the shop floor, they can also start into growth. A few green shoots may not be the end of the world and you can take a view as to whether the bulbs are still a good bet, depending on the time of year, the climate, your garden soil and your skill as a plantsman. But if the dry, rootless bulbs are a sorry mass of pallid etiolated shoots, reaching desperately towards the light, try to harden your heart. The chances of them establishing a healthy root system and growing away strongly are slim, and if they do survive, they may take years to put on a good display.

Pathetic as they may be, it is better by far to walk away and spend your hard-earned money on healthy, well-kept bulbs that will provide immediate gratification.

Buying potted lilies has advantages and disadvantages. The most obvious disadvantage is that it is a much more expensive way to buy the bulbs than purchasing them when dormant. This, however, may well be outweighed by the sheer pleasure of choosing the finest of the flowers available, and carrying them home to take up pride of place in the garden.

It is also an excellent way to fill gaps in the border, provide an instant, uplifting hit of color and to allow you to catch up with yourself if, for any reason, you didn't manage to plant bulbs earlier in the season. Furthermore, if the plant is in flower, you can be certain that it is the variety advertised on the label, since mix-ups in the packing shed can and do happen.

Planting lilies

Lily bulbs are frequently available in autumn and winter and are often also sold with other summer bulbs in the spring, but when is best, really best, to plant them?

Unfortunately, the answer is not always simple. Planting out your lily bulbs in autumn when they are fresh and juicy is one option, but it comes with the risk that they will suffer from cold and damp; they may fall foul of waterlogging or suffer the unseen depredations of slugs, which burrow between the scales beneath the ground.

Yet planting in spring comes with its own challenges. The lily wants to grow, so it may sprout in storage; the bulbs may dry and shrivel over the winter months, sapping the plant's energy and vigor and hindering its ability to establish well and put down roots fast when it is finally planted.

So, there is a tension. The risk of the bulb rotting in the wet must be weighed against the likelihood of it deteriorating in storage. What's more, this will vary from garden to garden and, indeed, year to year.

The essence of good gardening is understanding what the plant needs and providing for it to the best of one's ability. Certain bulbs are more tolerant of mistreatment than others and, rather like snowdrops, lilies do not like to dry out completely, while also resenting waterlogging, particularly when not in full growth. But once lilies are in the ground, happy and established, they will very often clump up nicely, the vigorous roots and strong sprouts dealing with the moisture with ease.

In a utopian situation, there is a strong argument for planting lily bulbs as early as possible – early autumn, in an ideal world – in order that the plant can get its roots down and start thinking about starting into growth. Its resources will not be drained over winter, and it is more resilient to future drought or excess moisture. And, when the weather warms and it starts to sprout, the healthy root system will be able to harvest water and nutrients from the ground and rapidly pump up the top growth.

But the world is not ideal, and if you find yourself with newly acquired lily bulbs, the best thing you can do is plant them either into a well-prepared border or – if the weather is cold and the soil soggy – into a pot to plant out again later. This way they don't dry out and you can protect them and cosset them until spring comes and conditions are more favorable.

Soil preparation

Prepare the soil before planting the bulbs by digging in leaf mold or compost, and perhaps a little grit on heavier soils – the heavier the soil, the more organic matter is required. This will retain moisture but allow good drainage. It is sometimes suggested that the bulbs should be planted on top of a layer of grit, or that a particularly gritty mixture should be used to backfill the hole, but the trouble with this is that on heavy soil it can create a sump – a nice porous pocket surrounded by impenetrable clay – which can fill up with water. So, essentially, your cherished bulb is sitting in a pond. Not good.

How deep to plant bulbs?

The rule of thumb with bulbs is to plant them at least twice as deep as the length of the bulb – measured from its basal plate to its crown. But, in fact, you can plant them more deeply still, which is particularly beneficial if the variety is tall, as it will offer greater stability, and with stem-rooting varieties.

The same rule should be followed when planting in pots – allow room for at least 4 inches of soil over the top of the bulbs.

The only exception to the rule is *Lilium candidum*, the Madonna lily, which prefers to be planted shallowly, with its nose just below the surface of the soil.

GROWING LILIES IN CONTAINERS

Lilies excel in containers, and if you are blessed with heavy, cold, clay soil or an unfavorable pH, this may be the best way to grow them.

For success, it is worth observing a few simple rules. First of all, choose a nice pot; it needs to have holes in the bottom for drainage and be heavy enough that it won't blow over in the wind. Whether this is a handsome container to take pride of place on the terrace, or a plastic pot that can be popped into the border or sunk into the ground is up to you, but the bigger the pot the more water and nutrients will be available to your bulbs, and the less likely it is to either dry out in summer or freeze in winter.

Aesthetically speaking, a large pot planted with five, seven or even eleven bulbs will be more dramatic and impressive than small pots with a more meager tithe of blooms.

When it comes to tricky soil conditions or fussy bulbs, pots have a range of advantages. The conventional approach is to fill the bottom of the pot with a good layer of crocks, then mix up a nice, heavy, loam-based compost, adding enough grit to ensure that it drains well. With this in place, you can add as much leaf mold or other organic matter to please whatever variety of lily you wish to grow.

To use lilies as house plants, bring them inside as the flower buds start to swell and site them in a cool, bright and airy location that does not get full sun. Avoid placing them near radiators or in very dry locations. Most problems arise from the soil being too dry or too wet, so check it regularly to ensure it remains moist, rather than soggy. Simply push your finger into the compost, up to the first joint; if it feels damp then it is fine, but if it feels dry give the plant a drink.

When growing lilies in containers, you will need to either incorporate a slow-release fertilizer or feed them regularly with a liquid feed, such as tomato food, when the plants are in growth. This is the case regardless of the variety you are growing, as the compost in a pot will not be replenished in the same way as will open soil. The pots can be overwintered in a frost-free place such as a shed or greenhouse, but since the key thing is to keep the compost dry, cover them with a bin bag or lay the pots on their sides to keep off the rain.

Care and maintenance

Once they get going, lily bulbs are hardy and reasonably low maintenance, but a little judicious attention will help to get the very best out of them, and staking, feeding and mulching at the right time will keep the display in tip-top condition, year after year.

Staking

If grown with shrubby neighbors, many lilies don't need staking, as the surrounding twigs will provide sufficient support. But if grown on a potentially windy site, by themselves in containers or among lax perennials, a stake can be a good idea.

The main risk with staking bulbs is that you may inadvertently spear them on the end of a bit of bamboo when pushing it into the soil, so add a short stake when the bulbs are planted, which can be swapped for a longer one as they grow. Other options include half-moon or bow-style stakes to stop the plants flopping forwards, circular supports or the conical frames designed to keep heavy-headed peonies looking perky.

Feeding and watering

Soils vary, and on a good, rich soil it may be unnecessary to feed or water the lilies to any great extent. But keep an eye on their growth and familiarize yourself with their habits. If the weather gets very dry, then give them a good soak all around the roots, preferably using stored rainwater. And if they seem a little lackluster, an application of high-potash liquid feed, such as tomato food, can give them a useful boost. Some fertilizers can cause leaf scorch, so feed and water the soil, not the leaves.

As ever, lilies are diverse, so get to know your plants and their behavior and preferences before lavishing them with nutrients. Some lilies, particularly those that evolved on poor soils, such as *Lilium regale* and *L. auratum*, do better when not too well-nourished.

Mulching

Applying a thick, fibrous mulch of organic matter in autumn and winter has several benefits: it discourages weeds by smothering them, and it improves soil structure, making it both more moisture-retentive and free-draining. A layer of mulch also insulates the soil and, eventually, rots down, in some cases freeing up nutrients that can be used by the plants.

Any organic material can work – shredded bark or bracken, spent compost, homemade compost, mushroom compost (although this can contain a fair amount of lime) and, the holy grail of mulchers everywhere, leaf mold.

If you have a few decent deciduous trees nearby it is easy enough to make leaf mold – just fill sacks with fallen leaves in autumn, piercing them to allow drainage, and leave them somewhere shady and out of the way for a couple of years. By this time, the leaves will have rotted down and become all soft and crumbly, ready to be spread on the soil.

Cutting back and deadheading

Whether or not you deadhead lilies is very much a personal thing. Removing the flowers means the plants are not allowed to set seed, so instead they channel all their energy back into their bulbs, ready for the next burst of growth. On the other hand, the seed heads can be an attractive feature and persist well into winter.

If you do deadhead for reasons of tidiness, preference or because you want to cut the flowers for the house or for showing, it is important to leave a good portion of the stem – a third to a half, at least – so that the leaves can nourish the bulb that remains.

In any case, the remaining dead stems can be removed at the end of winter, when clearing and tidying for the coming season.

Dividing lilies

Some lilies can stay put for decades with the absolute minimum of fuss, while others, despite the very best of care, are destined to bloom fleetingly, if brightly, before fading away. But when and if a clump becomes congested, it will be necessary to divide it. This will often reinvigorate the display with new growth and it also provides the opportunity to spread a favorite plant around the garden, providing a pleasing repetitive effect.

Dig up the clump, carefully, about four to six weeks after it has finished flowering, then gently tease the bulbs apart, replanting them as required (see page 217). The clump will be a combination of larger flowering bulbs and smaller ones that still need to grow on, and the latter can be given a bit more space to fatten up *in situ* or moved to another location, such as a nursery bed, to reach flowering size there.

Large clumps may have drained their immediate soil of nutrients over the years, so if it seems necessary, take this opportunity to dig in a bit of compost and improve the conditions into which you are replanting them.

Propagation

Lilies have a fundamental desire to increase in number and they can be quite astonishingly easy to propagate, either vegetatively or by seed. There are advantages and disadvantages in either case. Using seed can reduce the chance of spreading diseases, while the process of hybridization potentially allows new and improved garden forms to emerge. Vegetative propagation, meanwhile, enables a named cultivar to persist because the new individual is genetically identical to its parent, and it often yields a flowering plant more quickly than by sowing seeds.

Lilies by seed

Each seedpod can contain anything from one to hundreds of viable seeds, and although lilies tend to seed quite freely, some hybrids are more fertile than others.

Collect the pods when the lily has finished flowering and they have become ripe – for the early flowering lilies this can be around midsummer, but with later flowering types, such as many Trumpet and Oriental lilies, the seedpod may need to be harvested and taken indoors to finish ripening.

You can tell when the seeds are ripe by giving the dry pod a shake; if the seeds rattle, snap off the top and pour them out onto a piece of paper. Either sow the seeds immediately or store them in labeled envelopes, ideally in the fridge, to sow the following spring.

But in damp weather or late in the season, cut the stems bearing the seedpods about halfway up and hang them up over a piece of paper in a cool, dry and airy place such as a garage, dry shed or larder. As the seed ripens it will start to fall out and can be gathered up.

There are two types of seed germination in lilies:

Epigeal (above-ground germination) This takes place when the cotyledon (the first growth stage of the lily seed's embryo) grows up above the soil surface. As the root starts to swell, it forms a small bulb.

Hypogeal (below-ground germination) Here the cotyledon remains in the soil, forming a bulb that can spend some time developing and rooting, before the first true leaf emerges.

Either of these forms of germination can be immediate or delayed. Above ground, immediate germination is the most common, and while hypogeal-immediate germination can be treated in the same way, hypogeal-delayed germination can require sowing in warm soil, followed by a minimum six-week period of cool temperatures to nudge the seeds into action. General information on sowing lily seed is below, but it is wise also to check the specific requirements of the variety you are trying to grow.

Sowing lily seed

Sow into a pot or a tray of gritty, free-draining compost, covering the seeds lightly with ¼ inch of compost or vermiculite. Water the container from the bottom by immersing it in a shallow bowl of water, so as not to wash the seeds away, then place it into a plastic bag and twist the top to seal. Allow the seeds to germinate at room temperature, increasing ventilation by gradually opening the bag, as green leaves start to appear.

Once the seedlings are large enough to handle and have started to outgrow their container, prick them out and pot them up individually. As they get larger still, increase watering and feeding and grow them on in a cool, light and airy place.

The length of time it takes for the new bulb to become big enough to flower depends on the conditions and the individual species. In optimum conditions some species, such as *L. formosanum* and *L. philippinense,* can flower within a year, while Asiatic and Oriental hybrids will take two years and *L. martagon* will take at least four. The less congenial the growing conditions, the longer this process will take.

Vegetative propagation of lilies

The ways that lilies can replicate themselves are legion.

Bulb division The bulb itself will expand and produce daughter bulbs, often on an annual basis, in a similar way to other bulbs, such as daffodils. Vigorous clumps of lilies, with lots of new bulbs, will benefit from lifting and dividing every few years so that they don't get congested and run short of nutrients.

Separate large or congested clumps into sections or individual bulbs

Replant or pot up the divisions as required

Stem bulblets Stem-rooting lily varieties also produce small bulbs, underground, above the main bulb. These swell and produce their own roots; so, towards the end of the growing season, these can be detached and replanted to take on an independent life. Similarly, those species with wandering, stoloniferous stems will produce a few bulblets along their length, each year.

Stem bulbils Particularly prevalent in tiger lilies, bulbils are small, dark mini-bulbs that form above ground, in the leaf axils of the plant, swelling and producing roots before detaching to start life on their own. If you keep an eye on them, they are easy to remove when they are ready, and can be grown on to be planted out in the location of your choice.

Leaf buds and scales Removing single scales from a bulb and potting up each of these under sterile conditions can produce new bulbils, which can be useful if you want to produce a large number of new flowering plants in a short period of time. Detaching leaves from the stem, each with a small heel attached, and potting them up also yields new individuals in varieties, such as the Asiatics, *L. longiflorum* and *L. lancifolium*.

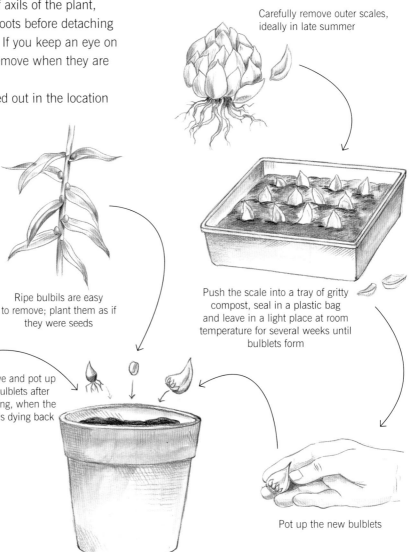

Carefully remove outer scales, ideally in late summer

Push the scale into a tray of gritty compost, seal in a plastic bag and leave in a light place at room temperature for several weeks until bulblets form

Ripe bulbils are easy to remove; plant them as if they were seeds

Remove and pot up the bulblets after flowering, when the plant is dying back

Pot up the new bulblets

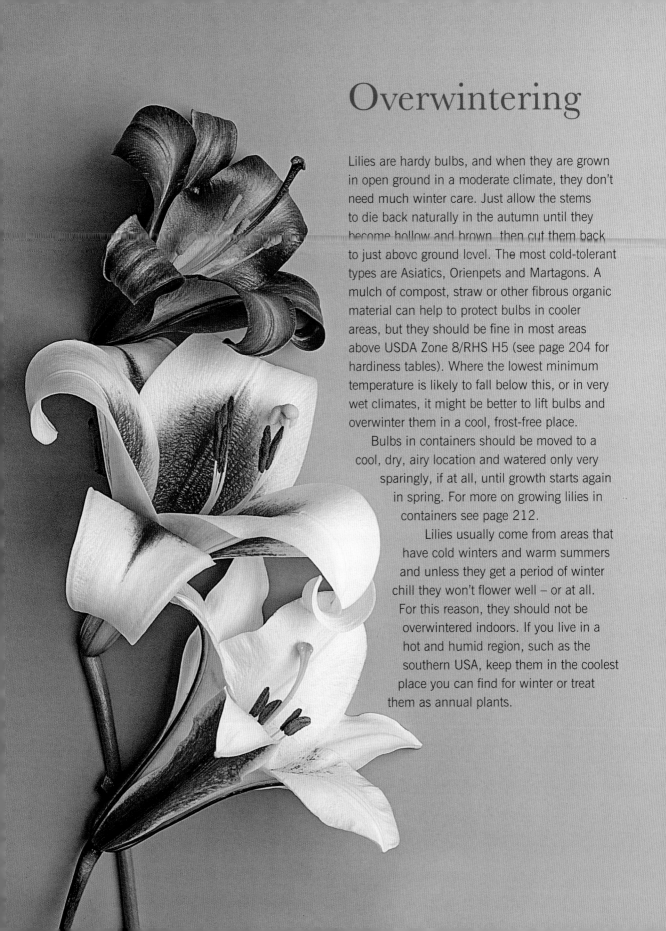

Overwintering

Lilies are hardy bulbs, and when they are grown in open ground in a moderate climate, they don't need much winter care. Just allow the stems to die back naturally in the autumn until they become hollow and brown, then cut them back to just above ground level. The most cold-tolerant types are Asiatics, Orienpets and Martagons. A mulch of compost, straw or other fibrous organic material can help to protect bulbs in cooler areas, but they should be fine in most areas above USDA Zone 8/RHS H5 (see page 204 for hardiness tables). Where the lowest minimum temperature is likely to fall below this, or in very wet climates, it might be better to lift bulbs and overwinter them in a cool, frost-free place.

Bulbs in containers should be moved to a cool, dry, airy location and watered only very sparingly, if at all, until growth starts again in spring. For more on growing lilies in containers see page 212.

Lilies usually come from areas that have cold winters and warm summers and unless they get a period of winter chill they won't flower well – or at all. For this reason, they should not be overwintered indoors. If you live in a hot and humid region, such as the southern USA, keep them in the coolest place you can find for winter or treat them as annual plants.

GROWING LILIES FOR SHOWS

Garden shows are one of the delights of summer, and it can be fun to exhibit as well as attend. Some growers take to competition with enthusiasm, vying for supremacy in a range of categories, to win awards, trophies and, most importantly, glory. Taking part is not usually limited to professionals and lily societies will have information about showing, including categories and presentation, on their websites or on request.

Once you have a copy of the rules, read and digest them, and under no circumstances make the mistake of thinking that they are guidelines – they are not. Follow them to the letter and you shouldn't go too far wrong: ignore them at your peril!

All elements of form, condition and quality are assessed by the judges and the stems (by which they mean the whole cut stem and flower ensemble) should be healthy and free of blemishes, and typical of the type of lily that you are presenting.

Practice and packing make perfect. Two or three days before the show, cut the flowers in the early morning cool. The stems should be long and the flowers should be at the point where the buds are starting to color. This bit is about timing: the flowers need to open in time for the show, and although expert tricks include putting them into warm sunlight or giving them a hot shower to speed them up a bit, there is a limit to what can be achieved if they are picked prematurely.

The next challenge is getting the flowers to the event intact, and every seasoned exhibitor has their own method. Try packing them in boxes with rolls of newspaper between the stems; slightly wilted plants will revive in water – their softness makes them resilient – but don't overdo it. Open flowers are more prone both to damage and to shedding pollen in transit, but for local shows, conveying stems in a bucket of water covered with a supporting mesh of chicken wire, or in a crate of bottles, one stem to each, can work. Take your very best blooms and some spares, too, just in case.

Bright, staining pollen can be a challenge, so some people cover the anthers with soft tissue paper, secured with a rubber band, for the purposes of transportation.

Once you get to the show and have found your spot, you must create a display that is a vision of beauty and perfection, so a little grooming is in order. Dead or damaged leaves must be removed, but dead leaf-tips and margins can be carefully reshaped and edited using a sharp pair of scissors, as can any dead or imperfect floral parts.

Brush dry pollen off leaves and petals with a soft brush; if it is wet, use a soft sponge dampened with water with a drop of soap in it. Should disaster strike, you may be able to carefully reposition a bent stem or re-angle a flower using florists' wire.

As the buzz intensifies and time runs out, take a final look. Check that you have set the display according to the strict judging criteria, size up the competition, then go and have a cup of tea. To display is a fine thing. To win is magnificent. But best of all is the chance to meet all the other lily enthusiasts, to find new friends and unusual characters, and to share the love of plants.

Pests and diseases

There is no royal road to our plants being untroubled by that which would eat or infect them, although, goodness knows, we aspire to it. Location, climate, plant variety, even the way in which your neighbors plant their gardens, can affect the things that you are trying to grow, and it is best to view pests and diseases as part of life's rich tapestry. But there are two things that make a huge difference to success: growing plants well so that they are strong and resilient, and being observant, to catch any problems arising. Remember this and you will face your potential gardening nemesis undaunted.

Pests

In some ways, the notion of a garden pest is tied up with the idea that one can be totally in control of the garden, that plants should be perfect and anything that challenges this nirvana should be battled and quashed. But this is a fundamentally flawed perspective and it sets us up for failure. Better by far to graciously accept our place in the ecosystem – and the fact that we are essentially laying on a buffet for other species – and moderate our actions accordingly.

LILY BEETLE
It is a pity that the lily beetle is a pest. It is a smart fire-engine red and it hangs out on the plants as if it owns the place. But its

handsome looks are let down by its atrocious manners.

Adult *Lilioceris lilii* grow to about 8mm (⅜ in) long and are often found in mildly orgiastic gangs, dropping to the ground if disturbed – not out of coyness, but because when lying on their backs they are camouflaged by their black tummies. Hatching from orange eggs, the grubs look like bird droppings, which is no real coincidence as they cover themselves with their own wet excrement. And although the lily beetle originates in Asia, it can now be found chomping its way through lily flowers around the world, so it looks like the scarlet recidivist is here to stay.

Lilies and their relatives can tolerate some damage from the beetle, but in severe cases this little pest can strip the plant back to its stalks, so it is well to be vigilant from mid-spring, earlier if it is warm, and remove all beetles, larvae and eggs by hand. How you dispose of them is up to you, but squashing missions are popular.

The larvae are more likely to be susceptible to pesticides than the adults and there are a number of organic insecticides on the market, but even these risk harm to both beneficial insects and innocent bystanders, so they should be avoided if at all possible. Other products are available, including one that claims to repel lily beetle by making the plant taste unappealing, while not harming other wildlife, which is a promising premise to work with.

SLUGS AND SNAILS
In the garden, mollusks are with us always. So rather than launching into an epic and rather Sisyphean battle of man versus slug, poisoning and contaminating the landscape and risking collateral damage to other animals, it can often be best to grow your plants so they are robust, hardy, and better able to withstand the odd nibble.

Yet it does not pay to be complacent. Early in the season, when lilies are just beginning to shoot, slugs can be a real problem, so be vigilant. Young and small bulbs can be easier to defend if grown on in pots and then planted out later, and tidying up around clumps in the ground can create a *cordon sanitaire*, devoid of places for slugs and snails to lurk.

A range of chemical treatments for slugs exists, but a targeted biological action is best for the garden ecosystem. Nematodes are sold by mail order as a solution to slug damage, and a dose of these mixed into water and applied to the soil in spring will thin out the pests and let the plants get away. In the meantime, cultivate a healthy population of blackbirds, thrushes and ground beetles, who will be more than happy to deal with slugs and snails for you.

MAMMALS

A number of mammals can disrupt a lily grower's bliss. The bulbs may be dug up by moles – this is disruptive but at least they don't eat them – or they can be a tasty snack for rabbits.

Barrier systems are often best – if the animal can't get to the plant the amount of damage it can cause is limited. Try growing the bulbs in aquatic baskets sunk into the ground and covering the tops with chicken wire. Or plant them in chicken-wire tubes, sunk well into the soil and surrounding the emerging stems. It is not a great look, but adjacent planting will soon disguise the wire defenses.

Note that lilies are extremely poisonous to cats; see page 27 for more details.

APHIDS

Sap-sucking greenflies, blackflies and their other aphid brethren are a common problem for many plants, and lilies are no different.

As ever, a well-grown plant is the best defense, and if you can just keep your hands in your pockets, sooner or later a whole host of ladybirds, lacewings and other predators will descend to sort them out, fueling the food chain and taking their place in the garden ecosystem.

If aphids become a real problem, the strong of stomach can squash them by hand, and there is a range of "organic" and soap-based treatments on the market for use *in extremis*. But remember, any chemical treatment for insect pests is likely to affect other insects, too – both the beneficial ones and those harmless creatures that just happen to be in the wrong place at the wrong time. Treatments should not be used on warm, bright days as they may harm bees and other pollinators, although, personally, I would be reluctant to use them at all.

Diseases

As there are no chemical controls available for lily diseases, prevention is far better than trying to do something about it once they have arrived. Make sure that the bulbs you buy are healthy, as the pathogens are often introduced when acquiring new stock. If you do find your plants have become infected, a prompt response and destroying any affected plant material, preferably by burning it, can help.

ROTS

There are a number of soil fungi that affect lily bulbs, including *Fusarium oxysporum* f. sp. *lilii* and *Rhizoctonia solani*. The first you are likely to know about it is when the leaves start to yellow – further investigation will often show that the bulbs are brown and rotting.

These fungi often enter the bulb through the basal plate, particularly if it is damaged, and affected bulbs should be removed immediately and destroyed. Do not grow lilies in that spot for at least five years, as the fungi persist in the soil.

Fusarium oxysporum f. sp. *lilii* is specific to lilies – although some species, including *Lilium henryi* and *L. superbum*, are said to be at least partially resistant. *Rhizoctonia solani*, meanwhile, is common and can affect a range of other bulbs, and plants, to a greater or lesser degree.

BOTRYTIS

"Lily disease" caused by the fungus *Botrytis elliptica* is a common problem in gardens. Oval brown spots appear on otherwise pristine leaves and these can spread and join up, in some cases affecting and destroying the whole leaf.

The fungus overwinters in dead leaf material and is transmitted by airborne spores that infect the plant in wet conditions. *Lilium candidum* and *L. regale* are especially susceptible, but no lilies are immune.

There is no chemical control and the best defense is to collect and destroy any affected leaves, to resist the fungus getting a foothold.

VIRUS

There are a number of viruses that affect lilies, and established clumps can often accumulate several different ones over time, so symptoms may vary.

One of the more common viruses – other than cucumber mosaic virus – is tulip breaking virus (TBV). This causes streaky, warped leaves and reduced flowering, while those flowers that are produced are also streaked and patchy and can fail to open properly.

As the name implies, this disease also affects tulips. Viruses are spread by sap-sucking aphids, so it can be a good idea not to grow tulips and lilies close together, to try to avoid cross-contamination. Affected clumps should be lifted and destroyed.

GLOSSARY

Anther The pollen sac at the end of the stamen.

Aurelian A term generally used for hybrids of trumpet lilies with *Lilium henryi*.

Basal plate The flattened stem at the bottom of the bulb structure which produces leaf scales above and roots below.

Bulb A rounded storage organ with a short stem and layered, fleshy scale leaves.

Bulbil A small bulb that develops above ground in the leaf axils of some lilies, particularly *L. tigrinum* cultivars.

Bulblet A small bulb formed underground, adjacent to the parent bulb.

Cotyledon In epigeal germination, the first leaf to emerge from a germinating seed, prior to true leaves.

Cultivar A cultivated form of the plant, selected for its desirable characteristics.

Deadheading Removing spent flowers from the plant to encourage more blooms.

Epigeal germination Seed germination where the cotyledon appears above the ground.

Forced, forcing A process by which a plant can be persuaded to flower out of season, usually achieved by modifying periods of cold and light exposure.

Heel The base of a cutting that has been pulled, rather than cut, from the parent stem leaving a small tail of material from the original plant.

Hybrid A genetic cross between two different species, genera or cultivars.

Hypogeal germination Seed germination where the seed produces a bulb first.

Leaf axil The joint between the leaf and the stem.

Ovary The enlarged basal portion of the female reproductive organ where seeds develop following fertilization.

Papillae Raised spots or bumps found on the petals of some lily flowers.

Pedicel A stalk that attaches a single flower to an inflorescence or main stem.

Perianth The outer, non-reproductive part of a flower, usually consisting of sepals (calyx) and petals (corolla).

pH The measure of acidity or alkalinity.

Plasticity The tendency of individuals of the same genetic makeup to look different from each other when grown under different conditions.

Potash The horticultural term for the element potassium (K) in water-soluble form – from the original practice of collecting wood ashes in a container.

Raceme An inflorescence where the flowers are spaced one above another to the top of the stem.

Recurved, reflexed Where the petals of a flower are curved backwards, often strongly so.

Rhizome Chunky, perennial rootstock which extends horizontally via new bulbs.

Scale Fleshy organs that make up a lily bulb; often used in propagation.

Species A population of individuals that has a high level of genetic similarity and that can interbreed.

Stamen The pollen-producing (male) reproductive organ of a flower. It consists of a filament and an anther.

Stigma The part of a flower's female reproductive organ that receives the pollen.

Stoloniferous In bulbs, the ability to produce bulblets at the end of a long, horizontally growing root stem, called a stolon.

Style The stalk or tube that links the stigma to the ovary.

Tepal Collective term for undifferentiated sepals and petals.

Umbel Type of inflorescence or flower head where several similarly sized flower stalks radiate from a common point.

Variety A classification of cultivated plants, below subspecies, where there are minor but distinctive and inheritable characteristics exhibited.

Vegetative propagation The process by which plants produce genetically identical new individuals or clones.

Viable (offspring) The progeny of a hybridization event between two fertile individuals, which are themselves fertile.

INDEX

TRADE DESIGNATIONS

Throughout this book each lily variety is referred to by its commercial name. In most cases the variety denomination in relation to worldwide Plant Breeders' Rights and any trade mark around the world relating to the commercial name has been omitted for ease of reading. The list below gives variety denominations and the trade mark status of the commercial names where applicable.

Lilium 'African Queen' (African Queen Group) (PBR)
Lilium 'Albufeira' (PBR)
Lilium 'Amarossi' (PBR)
Lilium 'Apricot Fudge' (PBR)
Lilium 'Beijing Moon' (PBR)
Lilium 'Candy Club' (PBR)
Lilium 'Distant Drum' (PBR)
Lilium 'Elodie' (PBR)
Lilium 'Exotic Sun' (PBR)
Lilium 'Heartstrings' (PBR)
Lilium 'Helvetia' (PBR)
Lilium 'Lady Alice' (PBR)
Lilium Lily Looks™ 'Sunny Azores' (PBR)
Lilium longiflorum 'White Heaven' (PBR)
Lilium 'Magic Star' (PBR)
Lilium 'Nymph' (PBR)

Lilium 'Perfect Joy' (PBR)
Lilium 'Playtime' (PBR)
Lilium 'Red Eyes' (PBR)
Lilium Roselily Anouska® = 'DI111067'
Lilium Roselily Elena® = 'DL04581' (PBR)
Lilium Roselily Natalia® = 'DL04544' (PBR)
Lilium Roselily Viola® = 'DL112838' (PBR)
Lilium 'Salmon Star' (PBR)
Lilium 'Saltarello' (PBR)
Lilium 'Soft Music' (PBR)
Lilium 'Sorbonne' (PBR)
Lilium 'Star Gazer' (PBR)
Lilium Trebbiano ('Gerrit Zalm') (PBR)
Lilium Triumphator = 'Zanlophator' (PBR)
Lilium 'Yelloween' (PBR)
Lilium 'Zambesi' (PBR)
Lilium 'Zelmira' (PBR)

AUTHOR'S ACKNOWLEDGMENTS

This book is dedicated to Morwenna Slade, for a mutual appreciation of things of beauty.

Beautiful, fragrant lilies have always intrigued me so to write this book was a thrill, but it was also a test of courage. It was created in a year of pandemic, against a backdrop of uncertainties, restrictions and concerns, but the result is simply wonderful and it has made me more thankful and proud than ever for the fabulous people I work and live with.

My husband and family have continued to be unswervingly supportive and it is only with the positivity and encouragement of Chris and our children that I achieve as many good things as I do.

Likewise, I must thank my friends and colleagues both in horticulture and the gardening media, and out in the wider world, for their kindness, advice and cheerleading whatever the season, weather or global crisis that currently besets us. Within this group, special mention must go to Guy Barter at the Royal Horticultural Society, who is always so generous and speedy with his wisdom, to Judith Freeman for her technical expertise, and the team at H.W. Hyde for helping with trade terms. I am most grateful.

I am indebted to Helen Brown at Little Ash Garden and Advolly Richmond, who proofread the copy and sent their comments, criticisms and compliments through in a variety of ink colors that made me laugh, even while I edited. You had my back and brightened up my day, too. Thank you.

Magnificent in adversity, it has been a joy to work with Lucy Smith, Helen Lewis and Isabelle Holton at Pavilion, while I am also grateful to Helena Caldon and Katie Hewett, who have made the editorial process smooth and easy. Thanks, too, to Somang Lee for her beautiful and informative illustrations and design dream-team, Alice Kennedy-Owen and Sophie Yamamoto.

In a year like no other, an enormous round of applause must go to my friend and colleague Georgianna Lane. Her ability to work photographic magic, pull pictures out of the ether and her tolerance for working in a supremely challenging situation never ceases to amaze me. With the help of her husband David Phillips, who should also take a bow, she has collected a truly magnificent selection of lily blooms for what is yet again a visually breathtaking book. In addition to being an absolute pleasure to work with, her eye and her professional rigor are a delight, and I look forward to our next project together.

PHOTOGRAPHER'S ACKNOWLEDGMENTS

My sincere thanks, as ever, to the team at Pavilion Books for conceiving this wonderful series and entrusting me to bring these exquisite subjects to life in photographs. For this title, I am indebted to Lucy Smith, Helen Lewis, Isabelle Holton and designers Alice Kennedy-Owen and Sophie Yamamoto.

Bravo and applause, once again, to my trusted friend and creative partner in this series, Naomi Slade, for her steadying presence and immense talent. As brilliant as any of the lilies depicted herein, Naomi's text engages and inspires, adding another dimension and elevating the whole with a generous dash of wit and sparkle that makes each specimen shine all the brighter.

Arlen Hill of Keeping It Green Nursery in Stanwood, Washington, provided priceless access to his important collection of early blooming Martagon lilies that otherwise would not have appeared here. At The Lily Garden in Woodland, Washington, Niels Van Noort contributed invaluable assistance and information, and we were honored to meet The Lily Garden founder and master hybridizer, Judith Freeman, who graciously contributed her expertise.

Tyler Meskers of Oregon Flowers in Aurora, Oregon, generously shared his knowledge and advice, and bestowed armloads of lavish cut flowers from his vast, state-of-the-art greenhouses. Kenn and Sylvia Parry of Parry's Tree and Lily Farm, LLC in Forest Grove, Oregon welcomed us to their beautiful hillside farm and nursery. A passionate plantsman, Kenn is a true artist when it comes to growing lilies, and many of his perfect blooms are featured in this book. Thomas Johnson and Kirk Hansen, of Sebright Gardens in Salem, Oregon, kindly shared their extensive knowledge and ensured I had early access to their glorious display garden at multiple times throughout the summer.

My appreciation, as always, to my patient and supportive family members, who well know, by now, that I will disappear down floral rabbit holes for months at a time each spring and summer.

Lastly, it is not overly dramatic to state that, without the dedicated contributions of my husband, David Phillips, this book would simply not exist. As a global pandemic shuttered location after location worldwide where I had originally planned to shoot (and sheer panic set in), he calmly and successfully undertook the urgent task of locating alternate lily growers, farms and gardens for me to photograph, and I'm certain actually conjured a few up out of thin air.

25 24 23 22 21   5 4 3 2 1

Published in the United States of America by
Gibbs Smith
PO Box 667
Layton, Utah 84041
1.800.835.4993 orders
www.gibbs-smith.com

Text copyright © 2021 Naomi Slade
Photography copyright © 2021 Georgianna Lane

ISBN 978-1-4236-5682-1
Library of Congress Control Number: 2020942001

Reproduction by Rival Colour Ltd., UK
Printed and bound by 1010 Printing International Ltd, China

First published in the United Kingdom in 2021 by
Pavilion
43 Great Ormond Street
London
WC1N 3HZ

The Publisher has made every effort to include all Plant Breeders' Rights
and trade designations. Should any corrections be necessary we would be
happy to make the relevant adjustment in any future printings of this title.

PICTURE CREDITS
PAGE 72: Jessica Hyde / iStock/Getty
PAGE 159: Clare Gainey / Alamy Stock Photo